100 Ideas for Primary Teachers

Developing Thinking Skills

Other titles available from Bloomsbury Education:

Breaking through Barriers to Boys' Achievement by Gary Wilson

Getting the Buggers to Behave by Sue Cowley

How to be an Outstanding Primary School Teacher by David Dunn

Once Upon an If by Peter Worley

The If Machine by Peter Worley

100 Ideas for Primary Teachers

Developing Thinking Skills

Steve Bowkett

B L O O M S B U R Y

Published 2014 by Bloomsbury Education

Bloomsbury Publishing plc

50 Bedford Square, London, WC1B 3DP

www.bloomsbury.com

978-1-4081-9498-0

A CIP record for this publication is available from the British Library.

1 3 5 7 9 10 8 6 4 2

Typeset by Fakenham Prepress Solutions, Fakenham, Norfolk, NR21 8NN

Printed by CPI Group (UK) Ltd, Croydon, CR0 4YY

This book is produced using paper that is made from wood grown in managed, sustainable forests. It is natural, renewable and recyclable. The logging and manufacturing processes conform to the environmental regulations of the country of origin.

To view more of our titles please visit www.bloomsbury.com

Online resources accompany this book available at:

www.bloomsbury.com/100Ideas-Thinking-Skills

Please type the URL into your web browser and follow the instructions to access the resources. If you experience any problems, please contact Bloomsbury at: companionwebsite@bloomsbury.com

To my wife Wendy who has always allowed me thinking time.

Contents

Acknowledgements

My thanks to my friend Tony Hitchman for his artwork and the many discussions we've enjoyed over the years. Thanks also to Sue Dixon of Thinking Child who has given me so many opportunities to think harder! Finally I want to acknowledge the enthusiasm and good humour of the children I've met on my school visits in allowing me to field-test my ideas. You have taught me so much.

Introduction

Thinking and learning go hand in hand. The more effectively children are able to think, the more they will understand the knowledge content of the curriculum and be able to link it to the world they live in and their own experiences. A further benefit of teaching thinking skills is that it helps to develop children's self-confidence and leads to raised self-esteem. Children that are more confident in their thinking are increasingly likely to 'have a go' when you ask for ideas and opinions or to play a more active role in group work and collaborative learning. They are also more inclined to question ideas and facts and will often ask for more information, both to deepen their understanding and out of interest. All of this will have a positive and long-lasting impact on the classroom environment.

This book offers a range of techniques and activities for showing children how to think in a variety of ways. The strategies and games can be taught individually or in combination and may be applied across the curriculum. You might use them as 'mind warm-ups' at the start of a lesson or they could form the substance of the lesson itself. However you choose to use these ideas, you'll find they work more powerfully if you keep the following points in mind:

- Make the thinking explicit. Explain to the children how the different kinds of thinking work. When children respond with ideas, point out to them how they are using their minds. Saying something as simple as, 'You've given me four ideas about what the person in the picture might be saying. That's a good bit of speculation' allows every child in the class to further their understanding of that skill.
- Value the children's thinking. They are still learning, so what might be an obvious idea to us could be a truly original insight to a child.
- Let the children do the thinking. That might seem an obvious point, but sometimes it's hard for us as adults not to jump in with the right answer or spoon-feed the children if we see them struggling.
- Model the behaviour. Let the children see that you're thinking about the problem too and that you don't always have the 'right' answer at your fingertips.

How to use this book

This book includes quick, easy, practical ideas for you to dip in and out of, in order to develop your students' thinking skills.

Each idea includes:

- A catchy title, easy to refer to and share with your colleagues.
- A quote from a teacher or child describing their experiences of the idea.
- A summary of the idea in bold, making it easy to flick through the book and identify an idea you want to use at a glance.
- A step-by-step guide to implementing the idea.

Each idea also includes one or more of the following:

Teaching tip

Practical tips and advice for how and how not to run the activity or put the idea into practice.

Taking it further

Ideas and advice for how to extend the idea, develop it further, or set it as homework.

Bonus idea

There are 14 bonus ideas in this book that are extra exciting, extra original and extra interesting.

Online resources accompany this book and can be accessed at www.bloomsbury.com/100ideas-thinking-skills. Also, share how you use the ideas in the classroom and join the conversation using **#100ideas**.

This is your brain

"I never knew you could get so many thoughts into such a small space!"

Giving the children some 'WOW' facts about the human brain is the first step in developing the classroom ethos of valuing thinking. It also helps children to realise that people think in many different ways and that there are various kinds of intelligence.

Ask the children to make their hands into fists and to hold them together in front of them, as if clutching something to look at it more closely. Tell them that this is roughly the size and shape of the human brain and that each hand represents a part, or hemisphere, of the brain.

Explain that the left part of the brain is more concerned with language, Maths and reasoning. It is the hemisphere where conscious thinking happens (thoughts I know I am thinking). The right part is more concerned with images, patterns, dreaming and making connections. In the right part, thinking is more subconscious: it occurs without 'me' realising that it does. When ideas occur 'out of the blue', or when we suddenly remember something, the thought has come from the subconscious to the conscious half. The left hemisphere has been called the 'scientist' part of the brain and the right hemisphere the 'artist' part. Now give the children some 'WOW' facts:

- The human brain is about 2% of our total body weight but uses around 20% of our energy. Thinking burns calories!
- Brain tissue is folded up in a very complicated way to pack it into your skull. The surface area of the brain is between 230-470 square inches.
- If you held a brain in your hands it would feel a bit squishy, like jelly. (Reference: www.brainhealthandpuzzles.com/)

Taking it further

Make a wall display featuring a picture of the human brain. Invite the children to research and add more 'WOW' facts. If you are a P4C (Philosophy for Children) school, combine these with related questions such as: Is the mind something different from the brain? What is a thought? Why do we dream?

The mind is like...

"This game is quick, simple and really helps children to realise how versatile their thinking can be."

Comparing the mind to people, places and objects gives children deeper insight into the range and power of their mental abilities.

Teaching tip

Run the activity again to consolidate the children's understanding of different kinds of thinking. So for instance if you focus on inferential thinking (for example, Idea 31 'Shoebox characters') you can round off the activity by saying 'So the mind is like a detective because...?'

To encourage children to get thinking about comparisons, introduce or revisit the idea of similes and metaphors. Explain that one benefit of making comparisons is to help us to understand difficult or abstract ideas. While the brain is a physical object or system, the mind is itself more of an idea. Making comparisons helps us to explore what it can do.

Use a few clear and obvious examples first. These might relate to other thinking activities the children have practised. For instance, you can relate the idea that 'The mind is like a spider's web because...?' to linking games that you have done previously with the class (for example, Idea 58 'Link to think'). But be careful here, with many creative thinking games, ideas are likely to come in a rush to begin with and then thin out. For each comparison, note the ideas and then explore them further afterwards.

So – the mind is like a spider's web because...?

Abby: 'Because it joins up all kinds of different thoughts and ideas.'

Ryan: 'Because I can sit in the middle and watch it thinking.'

Bita: 'Because the web doesn't make itself. *You* have to make it.'

John: 'Because it can keep getting bigger and bigger.'

Note: If you are a P4C (Philosophy for Children) School, some of the children's responses can serve as the starting point for a philosophical discussion. Ryan's reply for instance raises the interesting point about whether 'I' and the mind are the same thing or, if not, how they are related.

Develop the comparison game by asking each child to write down on a scrap of paper the name of an object, animal, person-related idea such as occupation, etc. Collect in the scraps and draw them out at random for the class to comment on. For example:

- 'The mind is like a crystal ball because it can imagine the future.'
- 'The mind reminds me of a butterfly. It can flutter from thought to thought but can also sit quietly in one place.'
- 'The mind is like the sea because it never stops moving.'
- 'The mind is like the TARDIS because it's bigger on the inside than on the outside.'
- 'The mind is like a treasure box that's full of precious things.'

A variation of this is to create a 6x6 grid of pictures (which the children can create using clipart, cut outs from magazines, drawings of themselves), then roll dice to choose images at random as points of comparison. Randomly selecting examples 'takes the mind by surprise' and encourages creative/spontaneous thinking rather than logical/analytical working out. (An example of a grid is available to download from the online resources.)

Taking it further

Highlight the idea that the word 'because' is related to reasons and reasoning. Explain that 'because' is a 'sticky' word: whenever it's used, you need to stick a reason on the end. This habit of thinking becomes useful during reasoned arguments and debates, for supporting and justifying opinions and for assessing the relative strength of multiple reasons.

Bonus idea ★

Create a class poem by asking groups to choose a number of examples to put together in verses. For example:

The mind is a butterfly because it flits from thought to thought,

It is a kitten because it loves to play.

The mind is a hive of bees, always busy,

The mind is a lion, strong, magnificent and proud.

Idea of the day

"A week after starting this, every child in the class wanted to contribute to the ideas board."

In this activity an 'ideas board' is set up and the children are invited to contribute to it.

Spend ten minutes each day talking about the chosen idea. An 'idea' (deliberately vague term!) can be a piece of factual knowledge, a question, an opinion, a joke, a puzzle to be solved, a mystery to wonder about, a piece of artwork, a photograph – anything that will engage the children's interest and encourage them to question, discuss, reason or do some research. Make it clear that all contributions are valued, from the ideas the children offer for display to their thoughts/reactions to what's on the board. It is also important for the children to realise that they don't have to offer an idea to go on the board, nor do they have to comment, if they don't want to.

Set up the ideas board with examples of your own. Ideas that work include:

- A picture of Van Gogh's Starry Night, with the question, 'Why didn't he paint the sky as it really is?'
- What if dinosaurs never became extinct? What problems might we have and how could we solve them?
- Pictures of famous people (alive and dead) together with the question, 'If you could meet just one of these people who would it be and why?'
- A selection of jokes. Ask the children to rate the 'funniness' of each on a 1-10 scale. Discuss why some people find a joke very funny while others don't laugh at all. What is humour anyway? Why do we laugh?

What could it be?

"I don't mind sharing my ideas in class now that I know there can be more than one answer to a question."

This is a quick and easy warm-up activity that allows children to generate and share ideas. It demonstrates the fact that even simple shapes and images can act as the basis for having lots of interesting ideas.

Put a large black dot on the board and ask the children, 'What could this be? What does it remind you of?'

- Acknowledge each child's idea as it comes along. Positive feedback helps to encourage less confident children to have a go, so you might say, 'That's an interesting idea' or, 'I hadn't thought of that before.'
- Lots of ideas will come along quickly but then children might start to struggle to think of more. Prompt them by saying (in this case), 'Think punctuation'. This serves to focus the children's thinking and will generate further ideas.
- Once the activity has run its course ask these questions: 'Out of the answers to my question, which is the right answer?' 'Out of all the ideas I've heard, which is the best idea?'
- It is likely that one or more of the children will reply 'All of them' or 'Any of them'. Your response to this should be encouraging, for example, 'That's a very wise thing to say.'
- Explain that you need to let yourself have plenty of ideas in order to have your best ideas and that this will help you to become a better thinker.

Teaching tip

This activity is a great 'thinking warm-up' at the start of a lesson. Doing it a number of times throughout the term will help children to realise that an important element of creative thinking is being able to look at things in many different ways.

Taking it further

After you have shown the children the black dot show the class images that are more complex to further thinking. To use the images again, turn them upside down. (Example images are available to download from the online resources for this book.)

Spot the difference

"This is a great mind warm-up to get us ready to learn."

'Spot the difference' is a quick, simple and versatile activity that helps to encourage the children's observational skills and develop their attention span.

Ask the children to 'spot the difference' in a variety of different ways. The complexity of the activity can be varied to suit the age range of the children, although you might well find that they will enjoy more difficult challenges rather than simpler ones.

- Use a graphics package to add/erase details from two identical pictures. Or you could show children pictures of two similar items, for example, insects, plants or shells, and ask them to *describe* the differences between them rather than just noticing them. Supply vocabulary as necessary. Children can also create a set of pictures for themselves as part of your ICT programme of work. (Two example pictures are available to download from the online resources.)

- Show the class two versions of the same piece of text with a number of differences between them: alternate spellings/misspellings, misplaced and missing punctuation and so on. Again, children could easily create these for themselves on the computer. This can be run as a whole-class or group activity, where children are invited to contribute orally or write down their observations. Differentiate the materials by giving different sets of clues according to ability.

Word links, chains and webs

"With this idea I found that I could put more rigour into teaching literacy *and* let children have fun with words!"

Use this activity as a quick and easy lesson starter or build it in to specific elements of your literacy teaching.

Word links and chains are a great lesson starter because you can use a variety of methods, for example:

- Rhymes: Try and create the longest chain you can using words that rhyme – dog, frog, log, hog, slog, blog and so on.
- Syllables: Make a word chain where the number of syllables increases each time. The words don't have to start with the same letter, though children like themes for example, using an animal theme: pet, kitten, elephant, rhinoceros, velociraptor.
- Rank order: Give the class a selection of words to put into an appropriate order – names of the planets in order of their position from the sun, names of towns or cities of increasing distance from your school, levels of size or complexity for example, word, phrase, sentence, paragraph, chapter.
- Links: Choose two apparently unconnected words and ask the children to create a reasonable link between them. This might be in the form of a word chain, a sentence or a drawing. For instance link 'paper' and 'happiness'. Possible 'chains' that connect these words include a thank-you letter, a ten-pound note, a favourite comic, a photograph of a friend or a drawing of a smiley face.

Taking it further

Creating association webs is an effective way of planning a piece of writing. Start with a word or picture stimulus and emphasise to the children that there are no set answers. Webs can be created in stages over the course of several days or even weeks, with children contributing as and when they want to. Alternatively, use the technique to practise brainstorming, where ideas are allowed to cascade out in two or three minutes. (An example of an association web is available to download from the online resources.)

Memory and imagination

"Learning to think well is like riding a bike – once you get the hang of it, it's easy."

Memory and imagination are fundamental resources for learning. Making children more aware of them is a key step in developing thinking skills.

Teaching tip

You may find that some children imagine colours easily but not sounds, or other variations of the 'dominant sensory mode' idea. Deliberately and repeatedly thinking of places, people and events in a multi-sensory way will help to enrich children's reading experiences and allow them to access more details mentally prior to writing.

Bonus idea ★

Ask the children to imagine a pleasant place and to make notes in response to questions such as, Are you seeing this place 'through your own eyes' as though you were standing there? Are you imagining colours and sounds? Can you notice textures and smells? Notice three interesting details now. What are they?

This simple activity can be done individually or in sequence with the bonus idea. They will be more effective if you practise them with the class regularly.

- Mind-body link: Point out to the children that our thoughts, feelings and bodies are connected. Ask them to remember a pleasant or funny experience. When they have done this, ask them to think about how they just reacted. Explain that smiling and laughing are physical reactions to the thoughts they have just had. Asking children to 'turn up' the colours and sounds of pleasant memories will make them even stronger.
- We tend to remember events in the same way each time, including unpleasant experiences. If a child is upset by their memories, sit with them and ask them to deliberately bring the memory to mind but to also *change* it. This could be changing the colours they recall, altering the sound of people's voices or putting a cartoon character in the middle of the memory. The aim is to give the child a greater sense of control over thoughts and feelings they would rather not have. Practising this technique repeatedly makes it much more effective.

Notice your thoughts

"We all have a rich inner world of imagination that we could enjoy so much more using a few simple techniques."

Practising this technique five minutes each day can improve children's experience of reading and raise the quality of their writing very quickly.

The ability to notice and manipulate your own thoughts is termed 'metacognition', or 'thinking about thinking'. Daily practice of this skill will make a significant impact.

- Give the class a sentence such as, 'Jones lay slumped on the sofa.' Ask the children to tell you what they're thinking or to jot down their ideas. Ask them what they think Jones looks like, for example, details about clothes and hairstyle. Many children will assume that Jones is a man, but there is no evidence for that in the sentence. This creates the opportunity to talk about assumptions. Point out too that the word 'slumped' carries a lot of information: we can picture exactly how Jones is positioned. Emphasise that the words children choose in their own writing is an important part of the process.
- Take the technique further by using metacognitive reading. Read a short extract from a story and encourage the children to notice their thoughts – for example, sights, sounds, smells – as you read. Give each child a copy of the extract to paste in the middle of a large sheet of paper and then ask them to add notes about the details they imagined. Practising this technique allows children to access more details during their thinking/planning time prior to writing.

Teaching tip

If when you ask for more details about Jones a child replies 'I don't know' say, 'Well pretend you do and tell me when you know.' This little trick will usually get a positive result.

Taking it further

In their writing many young writers use the first ideas to pop into mind or the first/most obvious details that they have imagined. Taking just a few more moments to create alternative ideas or to notice more details will make the children's writing more original and will give them more to write about.

Paying attention

"It's amazing how much we don't notice until we start paying attention!"

Paying more attention is an easily learned skill that underpins more effective thinking and all the benefits that it brings.

The ability to direct and focus our conscious point of awareness is a powerful aspect of our thinking. Practise it regularly with your class. Here are a few simple activities you can try out:

- Ask the class to become aware of their own bodies. Notice the weight of their body on the seat and the feeling of their feet resting on the floor. Notice their hands and they way they're folded together or the texture of the surface underneath them. Now ask them to notice their own breathing. Explain that usually we just 'let' breathing 'happen', but it is easy to slow and deepen the breathing and this helps us to relax.
- Ask the children to notice any areas of tension in their body and deliberately relax them. Unwrinkle a frown. Let tense shoulders loosen. Let a tense stomach 'slump'. If they are twitching a leg, tapping toes or fingers, see if they can stop it.
- Get the children to close their eyes and imagine the classroom. After a minute or so open eyes and look around. What had they failed to bring to mind because they'd never noticed it?
- Split the class into pairs or groups of three. Give each group an interesting object – a shell, flower or stone – and ask the children to spend a few minutes *really* noticing its details. There doesn't need to be any other outcome to this activity, but children often enjoy telling each other or writing down what they've noticed.

Taking it further

Show the class pieces of artwork and enjoy a few minutes' quiet 'noticing time'. Play suitable music and ask the children simply to notice the complex melodies. Again, there need be no other outcomes apart from the enjoyment of appreciation.

Focussing five senses

"When your imagination improves, thinking of things to write about is easy."

Multi-sensory thinking combined with observational skills helps to improve children's reading and writing. It also has benefits for learning right across the curriculum.

We take in information through all of our senses. Subsequently, when thinking of the world in our imaginations, we tend to rely more on one sensory mode than the others. For instance, a more visually-oriented child will tend to think in images, which are usually coloured, and would need to make more of an effort to hear imagined sounds or feel imagined textures. Developing multi-sensory thinking can redress this balance and lead very quickly to more richly detailed work.

- Ask the children to close their eyes and notice sounds nearby. After a short time, ask them to notice more distant sounds, before paying attention again to sounds that are closer.
- Give each child a small everyday object. Again with eyes closed, ask them to really notice its shape, size, weight and texture.
- Pick a colour and ask the children to notice as many shades of it in the room as they can.
- Ask children to note down their thoughts in response to questions such as:
  - What does milk look like as it's poured into coffee or tea?
  - Describe your favourite flavour as exactly as you can.
  - Imagine plunging your hands into a bucket of flour. What does that feel like?
  - What sounds do the raindrops make on the roof and windscreen of a car?

Teaching tip

Increase the benefit of listening to sounds that are nearby or far away by asking children to notice each aspect of them. Ask them to pay attention to direction, volume, pitch, tone and length (continuous or intermittent).

Observation journal

"I like my journal because I can do all kinds of writing in it and just write a little bit if I want to."

An observation journal is a versatile tool for familiarising children with a range of different forms of writing.

A further motivation is to employ what I call the 'minimal writing strategy', where you suggest the children can just make brief notes or write only a few sentences if they wish. The only condition is that they must think about what they want to say and choose their words carefully. Reluctant writers are more likely to try this due to this 'good deal'.

Observation journals can contain entries based on some of the other ideas in this book (for example, Ideas 15-20 on multi-sensory thinking, Idea 42 'A cloud of questions' and Idea 91 'Annotated notebooks', where children can reflect on their own previous observations). Encourage children to notice the world around them: the weather, plants, insects, people and places. Writing can take place at any time, though it's best to record observations as they happen. Model the behaviour by keeping an observation journal yourself.

- Observation journals work best if you suggest to the children that they don't need to show anyone what they have written if they prefer not to.
- Consider not marking the work unless a child specifically asks you to. Even then you can mark selectively — just for spelling perhaps or only for punctuation. Alternatively, you can write a personal response to the entry while ignoring technical inaccuracies. For some children this takes the worry out of 'committing' themselves to paper: they can concentrate on what they want to say without trying to remember a raft of rules at the same time.
- That said, if a child is happy for you or their classmates to look in the journal, suggest that they designate one or more pages as 'public' pages, in which case they must do their best to make the work as neat and accurate as possible.

Picture this

"Your imagination is like a horse. With training it won't run away with you – in fact, you can take it wherever you want it to go."

This activity develops the children's ability to visualise and internalise their attention while increasing their concentration span.

Show the children a picture of a detailed scene, preferably in black and white, and ask them what they notice (an example scene is available to download from the online resources). Then ask the children to 'manipulate' the image in their minds, and tell them that after approximately 30 seconds of thinking time you are going to ask them to make brief notes for each of the following tasks:

- Change point of view: Become one of the people in the picture. How does the scene look from that perspective?
- Move beyond the frame: Imagine what's along the street, around the corner?
- Add characters: Imagine you can see the faces of some of the people. What do they look like?
- Overview: Pretend you can float up and look down at the town with a bird's eye view. What do you notice?
- Jump time: Imagine the scene in motion, then slow everything down. For instance, using the picture from the online resources, pretend the man on the left is carrying samples of glassware in his suitcase. The case pops open and glasses and paperweights fall to the ground and shatter. Observe how 'slow-motion thinking' gives you time to notice even more details.

Teaching tip

A key element of developing thinking skills is to make thinking explicit. So, again using the example picture available to download, if one response to a picture of two people sitting in a car is 'I think the people in the car are arguing', ask what clue or clues the children noticed to come to that conclusion? Obviously, in this case, the fact that the people in the car are looking at each other, both with mouths open as though shouting, is a big clue. Explain that looking for clues that support an idea is called 'inferring'. Help children to practise this by asking further questions such as, 'How do we know the traffic lights are red?' or, 'How do we know the woman with the children does not want to go into the shop?'

First impressions

"Doing this activity helps me with my story writing and it makes me a better thinker too."

This simple technique makes children more aware not only of their thinking but also of the idea that their thoughts and feelings are connected. Use this idea as a starter game in conjunction with other thinking activities found in this book.

Teaching tip

This activity is a useful way of helping children to generate ideas for their own stories. Also, the process of reflecting on first impressions can be transferred to other kinds of writing (for example, persuasive writing, argumentative essays) and is useful in helping children to become more 'emotionally intelligent'.

Show the class a picture and ask the children to jot down their first impressions. (See the online resources for an example of a picture to show.) You are likely to glean a range of responses, which then form the basis of further activities. For example, show a picture of a man walking through an alley at night, clutching a bag and looking over his shoulder; here are some thoughts the children may have:

- 'He's being followed. I think he's stolen some jewellery and it's in that little bag he's holding.' There's opportunity here to look at inference and speculation. We can infer from the way the man is glancing behind that someone is following him (though we don't know for sure). And maybe there are jewels in the bag. Ask what else it might contain.
- 'He's hurrying along this really creepy-looking street...' With a response like this, ask what clues the children notice that create the impression that the man is 'hurrying' and that the street is 'creepy looking'. By asking them to focus their attention this way, you are helping them to make explicit and to explain observations that they might otherwise never have thought about further.
- 'I think he's a criminal. I don't trust him.' Here we have an observation linked to an opinion and a thought linked to a feeling – an example of an 'obserpinion' (see Idea 33).

Catch yourself on

"I explain to my class that someone's imagination is like a horse. If you don't control the reins, it can run away with you."

An Irish friend of mine uses the expression, 'catch yourself on' to mean 'get a grip of yourself'. *Catch Yourself On* would make a useful poster in your classroom when it comes to teaching thinking skills.

I often explain to children that the mind is like a toolbox – it is filled with all kinds of amazing tools and gadgets for thinking, imagining, feeling, moving – and that being an effective thinker means knowing which tool to choose for which job. Being more self-aware is one of the most powerful of them.

Present the class with situations such as the ones below and say, 'What do you think is happening here?' or, 'How do you feel about this?' Note: It isn't necessary for the children to tell you what they think; what's important is that the children reflect on their first (and maybe automatic) impression.

- You see a man in a hoodie running down the street clutching a woman's handbag.
- You notice a very overweight person coming out of a cake shop smiling.
- You see two people looking in your direction. One of them laughs.

It's easy to make assumptions and jump to conclusions. For example, did anyone assume that the boy in the hoodie had stolen the woman's handbag? What assumptions did they make about the overweight person? Or, if any children thought they were being laughed at, ask the class to think of other reasons why the person might have been laughing. This is a good opportunity to explore generalisation and stereotyping.

Teaching tip

Regular practice of 'catching yourself on' will hone the skill and teach children to think twice about jumping to conclusions. Run the activity often and encourage the children to apply it more generally in their lives.

Colourful thinking

"Playing this game makes the world a more colourful place!"

Developing visual thinking can help children's reading and spelling as well as their creative writing.

Look again at the picture of the walking man from Idea 13 'First impressions'. Show this (or another black and white) image to the class and say, 'Pretend this picture is in colour. *Turn up* the colours in your imagination and when you've noticed at least one colour, tell me the colours you can see.'

- Notice how the instruction is framed. 'When' is a presupposition of success, so subconsciously children will note your high expectation that they will be able to carry out the task. Telling them they *will* notice at least one colour reinforces this view.

- Some children – the more visually-oriented thinkers – will respond immediately, but even those that have difficulty imagining colours are being given the opportunity to practise the skill, which will develop over time. As children respond, ask for more details. If a child says the man's tunic is blue, ask what kind of blue. If someone else then says the sky is blue, ask how that colour blue is different to the blue of the man's tunic.

- Look out for children who say things like, 'The roof tiles could [or should] be red, because tiles often are.' In this case they are not imagining colour but 'working it out logically'. I tell them not to use could/should but to *turn up* the colours in their mind's eye and tell me when they can see them.

Now listen

"Most children become wonderfully quiet when they are listening to the sounds in their minds!"

Developing auditory thinking has immediate benefits for boosting listening skills and other areas of children's learning.

Again using a black and white picture, ask the children to: 'Turn up the sounds. Listen to the sounds coming out of the picture and when you've heard at least one you can tell me about them.'

- Notice what happens. Some children – the more 'auditory-oriented thinkers' – respond at once. Some children who can imagine colours now have nothing to say: they haven't developed the skill of hearing 'sounds' from pictures. Others in the class will be able to imagine colours and sounds.
- As responses come along, ask for more detail. If a child says, 'I can hear the rats squeaking,' ask them to listen more closely – what other sounds do the rats make?
- In running this activity, encourage the children to play with sounds and to speak them aloud. This will help them to become more familiar with phonics and the phonetic structure of words. Encourage the children to make connections between words in terms of phonetic similarities – 'scratch', 'scrape', 'scrabble', 'scritch'; 'crack', 'crackle', 'crinkle', 'crumble'.
- Explore the finer details of sounds – direction, volume, pitch, tone. This leads on to children making more subtle distinctions. For instance, imagine dropping three similarly sized pebbles into three puddles. One goes 'splish', one goes 'splash' and one goes 'splosh'. What's the difference between the puddles?

Teaching tip

As children speak many will use physical movement to help them imagine the sounds. For example, children will frequently make clawing movements for sounds such as 'scratch' and 'scritch'. Explain to them that physically acting out a sound can help them to imagine it more vividly and to appreciate it more.

Taking it further

Using everyday objects and musical instruments, have the children create sounds and then name and describe each one. Encourage the invention of new words and phrases. A child might describe dropping some pencil erasers onto a table as making a 'rubbery dubbery dub dub dub' sound.

17

Jump in

"When we do this game it helps me to stop fidgeting."

Practising 'tactile thinking' reinforces the idea of the mind-body link. It also makes children more body-aware and develops their appreciation of the world around them.

Teaching tip

Link tactile imagination to an increasing awareness of and ability to describe feelings. If a child says, 'The man feels nervous', say, 'What does being nervous feel like in your body?' Open it out to the class, 'How would you explain to someone who has never been nervous what that actually feels like?'

Taking it further

Bring in a variety of objects and materials for the children to touch. How would they describe those textures? Similarly, let the children smell various spices and herbs. How would they describe those aromas to someone who has never smelled them? See Idea 18 'The colour of saying' for more advice on this.

Once you have used a picture to imagine colours and sounds, ask the children to: 'Step into the picture. Stand *in* that place and you will notice some new things.' In doing this you have helped the children to experience another aspect of their imaginations. Many will now respond with impressions of temperature, texture and smell, often accompanied by body movement − a child might shiver and hug themselves as they tells you it's cold in that street. Another might wrinkle their nose as they reports that the alley smells bad.

- Encourage all of the children to explore their imagined world in a tactile way, to deliberately reach out and touch walls and windows. Feel the chill and dampness in the air. Can anyone come up with a more detailed description beyond simply saying it was a 'chilly damp night'? What is the *particular quality* of the air at that moment?
- This offers a great opportunity to revisit simile and metaphor. Examples children have given me to describe 'cold' include, 'It was like tiny icy particles settling all over your face'; 'The cold made your head ache as though someone had thumped you'; 'It was a heavy, cruel cold like a sack on your shoulders.'

The colour of saying

"When I learned this trick I found I could describe loads more things in interesting new ways."

Cross-matching sensory impressions quickly boosts the children's ability to describe sights, sounds and textures in more powerful and original ways.

On one occasion I was running a writing workshop with a Year 5 class, using a black and white picture of a bonfire scene. I asked the class to 'jump into the picture' (see Idea 17 'Jump in') and one child, Ellie, immediately sniffed the air and said, 'Oh I can smell the fireworks!' I replied, 'Pretend I've never smelled fireworks before, Ellie. How would you describe the smell now so that I can smell it too?' She thought for a while, struggling to gather the words together, and eventually told me that it was 'quite a nice smell'.

I wasn't going to leave it there. I said, 'Pretend you can touch the smell. What does it feel like?' 'Soft and fluffy like cotton wool.' I asked her to imagine the colour of the smell, then to pretend the smell was a sound. We ended up with 'The fireworks have a soft, fluffy, whispery light purple smell,' which was a far more vivid and original response than 'quite nice'.

Most children will quickly pick up the knack of describing one sensory impression using vocabulary usually associated with other senses. This happens in our language anyway. For instance – austere, big, crisp, earthy, firm, green, lean, sharp, silky, steely, undertones – are all terms used by wine connoisseurs to describe the smell and taste of wines.

Once children have grabbed this insight, their descriptive writing will become far more evocative and original.

Taking it further

Play some instrumental music. Say to the class, 'If these sounds were a person, what would that person look like?' After the children have responded, play the music again and say, 'If this music was their personality, what kind of person would they be?' Or, show the class a piece of abstract art and ask, 'If this picture was music, what would you hear?'

Thinking journeys

"Thinking journeys are a great way to show children that they all have imaginations and that these can become more powerful and effective with training."

This activity helps children to notice their own thoughts, thereby developing concentration and metacognitive skill. It can also improve children's vocabulary and descriptive writing.

A thinking journey is a guided visualisation. Explain to the children that there is no 'right answer' to the questions you ask: what is important is that each child thinks carefully about the words they choose to describe their mental impressions.

Explain to the children that you are going to ask them to imagine they are going on a journey. Every so often, you'll stop and ask them a question and they can write down their response – no more than a sentence or two. They don't have to 'answer' every question. After each question, allow a minute or so for thinking and writing time. Make sure your questions help children to 'think with all of their senses' (see Idea 20 'Use all of your senses'). Here is an example visualisation:

Taking it further

Thinking journeys can be brief: using this technique for a few minutes after playtime helps children to settle and get ready to learn. Longer visualisations can be used as a precursor for more extended descriptive writing. When children have done several thinking journeys, invite them to write their own to use with their classmates.

- Pretend you have driven a car down to the beach. Just as you turn off the engine there's a heavy shower of rain. Imagine I have never heard that sound. Can you describe it to me? (Tip: Discourage obvious or cliché responses such as pitter-patter and splish-splash.)
- You cross a wide strip of pebbles barefoot. What does that feel like?
- You buy some candyfloss. Describe the smell and taste and texture to someone who's never eaten it before?

Use all of your senses

"After practising multi-sensory thinking for a few weeks, one girl in the class said it felt like taking a paper bag off her head!"

Consolidate the sensory work you've been doing with the class by trying out these activities.

Once I asked a Year 6 group to write a description of eating a piece of fruit.

- The teacher took me aside and said that one boy, Cameron, probably wouldn't do it because he didn't like writing. When I looked, Cameron had thrust his fists into his armpits and seemed to be sulking – though when I next glanced over I realised he wasn't sulking but staring at something invisible on his table. Then he reached out, picked it up, sniffed it, felt its weight, rubbed it on his shirt, bit into it (wiping the juice off his chin), put it back down and wrote the best description of eating an apple in the whole class. When I asked him how he had managed to write such a mouth-watering description he said, 'Well you've got to put your whole self "in" to get the right words "out".' I remind children to do this because your imagination goes all the way through you.
- Ask the children to write a short description using all their senses.
- Encourage the children to make notes in their observation journal (see Idea 11 'Observation journal') as far as possible using all of the senses.

Taking it further

Apply multi-sensory thinking to feelings. With pleasant feelings, imagine they have colours, sounds, shapes and textures and 'turn them up' to make them brighter, louder, stronger. When working with unpleasant feelings, do the opposite – shrink them, change the shape, bleach out the colours, mute the volume, smooth off the rough edges. Finally, imagine the whole thing and 'catch yourself on' (Idea 14) by thinking of the feeling in its modified form from now on.

Visualising

"Imagination is more important than knowledge." Albert Einstein

Visualising is a key skill that brings benefits to all areas of a child's learning.

Taking it further

If you repeat the 'Incremental changes' activity, steadily increase the time that the children have to concentrate on making changes. To round off the activity, ask them to imagine an overview of the whole car with all the changes they have made.

Bonus idea ★

Visualising is a useful skill when it comes to enhancing the richness of children's creative writing. The more details they can imagine, the more 'raw material' they have to write about. Encourage the children to imagine characters, places and objects in as much detail as they can; allow enough thinking time for this. Prompt them with questions (but resist giving them ideas). A question such as 'And what other two interesting things do you notice about …?' often comes in handy.

Imagination has been defined as the mental ability to move beyond our present circumstances. By an act of imagination we can mentally visit other times and places, make plans, envision our future and, by wondering 'what if', consider a range of possibilities that do not yet exist. Along with memory, imagination powers the human mind and constitutes a life-transforming resource.

Visualising allows us to practise the skill of deliberately linking thoughts and constructing mental scenarios. Try these activities with the children before inviting them to come up with other ideas of their own:

- Describe the route: Have the children working in pairs. Ask one of them to visualise a familiar route, say from home to school or the shops, and to describe it to their partner. The partner can ask questions or request more details, though this should be done with a light touch so as not to interrupt the visualiser's flow of thoughts.
- Incremental changes: Ask the children to imagine an object they all know, for example, a car. Describe a car to them in detail or show them a picture. Then go through a checklist of small changes that you want the children to make to the imagined vehicle: turn the tyres pink, imagine sitting in a different seat in the car, change the radio stations, etc. The children can work in groups for this or you can run it as a whole-class activity.

Be nosy

"Our teacher encouraged us to be nosy, but said that doesn't mean asking personal questions!"

To 'be nosy' means noticing and questioning. These are behaviours that form the core of a thinking skills agenda in any school and are the basic outcomes of natural human curiosity.

Noticing and questioning are embodied in most of the activities in this book, but together they form an attitude that should be encouraged in all children and an ethos of curiosity that informs the way our children are taught.

Although noticing and questioning are natural behaviours, they can easily be dampened if children's thinking is not valued or, for convenience or to save time, we want them to be passive recipients of facts rather than active interrogators of the information presented to them. Your whole classroom and teaching style can be oriented towards cultivating 'nosiness'. Here are a few ideas to kick-start the process:

- Put an interesting object on your table every few days – an intriguing device or implement, a piece of exotic fruit, a puzzling picture and so on.
- Make a poster for your room that says, 'What brilliant question will *you* ask today?'
- If a child asks you a question and the answer does not come immediately to mind, feel confident in saying, 'I don't know, but how could we find out?'
- Set up a thought-for-the-week display space on your wall. In the centre you can put a quote, a proverb, a 'WOW' fact, or an intriguing picture. Invite children to add their own responses in the form of opinions, related facts and further questions.

Teaching tip

Model the behaviour. When you make a point of noticing and questioning, the children will feel more comfortable and confident to be like that too.

Taking it further

Apply the children's emerging observational skills in other areas. Focus their attention on the particular language they use when referring to themselves and each other. Point out how small details of facial expression and body posture offer insights into how someone may be feeling. In this way, training observation helps to develop empathy.

States of mind

"I never realised before how the way I think can affect my moods."

Our thoughts, feelings and physical behaviour are linked. Making children more aware of how their minds work helps them to become more emotionally resourceful.

Here are some tips and techniques for helping children to get ready for learning:

- Give them some 'quiet breathing time' before delivering new ideas or asking them to recall previous facts. Show children how to breathe in a controlled way – ask them to breathe in while you slowly count to four, hold for another count of four and breathe out slowly to a count of four.

- Use anchoring techniques to help children access positive moods and beneficial learning states. An 'anchor' is a link that develops between a behaviour you want the children to display and something you have under your conscious control. A very elegant example is where you designate a space in your classroom where you always stand to introduce new ideas, facts and topics. There's no need to tell the children about this anchor spot: they will subconsciously form an association between you being there and being ready to listen and think. See Idea 50 'Anchor the learning' for more details.

- Be aware of assimilation time, waiting time, and thinking time. All of us need time to process or assimilate new information. When you have given the class some new facts and ideas, it will take the children time to integrate them with what they already know. Review the learning later that day or the next day. When you ask children questions, allow them a decent length of time to frame their response and don't feel tempted to jump in quickly with the right answer.

Taking it further

During 'breathing time', as children inhale, ask them to visualise breathing in a white light. This light is full of energy and enthusiasm and gets the mind ready to learn. As they exhale, ask them to visualise a blue light. This washes away all the worries and concerns they may have and all the stresses and strains of the day. White-light-blue-light breathing is an ancient technique that is sometimes used in conjunction with the practice of meditation.

Making patterns

"Sometimes the best ideas come along when you're not trying to have them."

Two key elements of creative thinking are making connections and looking at things in different ways.

Making connections happens both subconsciously and consciously, when we take two or more previously disparate ideas and link them, thereby creating new information, but think of it as two words: *in formation*. Taking multiple perspectives on ideas keeps our thinking flexible and fresh.

Here are some activities for cultivating creativity:

- Show the children a big black dot and ask, 'What could it be? What does it remind you of?' Ideas are likely to come in a rush. As they thin out, prompt further thinking by saying, 'Now think punctuation...' 'Now think animals...' (See Idea 4 'What could it be').
- Give out sheets of paper speckled with dots together with a theme such as animals, constellations, dinosaurs, etc. Ask the children to join the dots to create as many examples as possible.
- 'Pareidolia' is the technical term for the tendency we have to see faces, animal shapes and so on, in clouds, in flames in the hearth and in other objects. Search on Google image for 'pareidolia' and you will find lots of examples to show the children.
- Ask each child in the class to write down on separate scraps of paper the name of an object, animal or feeling. Put them in an envelope then draw out two at random and ask the class to come up with as many reasonable links between them as they can.

Taking it further

Follow up these activities by asking, 'Out of all of the ideas you've given me which is the right one?' At least one child is likely to say, 'Any of them', if not, try to elicit this answer from them. Then ask, 'And out of the ideas I've heard from you, which is the best one?' Again, you're looking for 'Any of them.' Point out to the children that the name of the game is how many different ideas can we have, and the use we make of them.

A thinking audit

"I never realised that we could do so many different kinds of thinking."

A key component of developing effective thinking in children is to make the thinking explicit, to bring it out into the open.

Teaching tip

Have quotes about thinking and the mind up in your room. A quick internet search will give you plenty of examples.

Here are some activities to facilitate effective thinking:

- In the same way that you might have definitions of mathematical ideas, grammatical terms, reading levels and writing levels up on your wall, create a display of different kinds of thinking. A typical 'thinking' poster will have the name of the skill, a definition/explanation and at least one example or activity for the children to try out. For example, 'Hypothesising. A hypothesis is an attempt to link together or explain things we have noticed about the world. What explanations can you think of for these...?
  - The way the Moon's phase changes from night to night.
  - The fact that cheese left out in the open goes mouldy.
  - The fact that the leaves of some trees turn brown and drop off in the autumn.
  - The fact that rainbows don't last long.'
- Notice the language children use that reflects the thinking they have done and point it out to the class. For instance, look again at Idea 15 'Colourful thinking'. In imagining colours you'll often hear a child say, 'I imagine that the sky is kind of bluish, blackish...' Your response could be, 'I like the way you've given us two colour words to think about. And I notice what you did to the ends of those words. (To the class) What do you think the difference is between something that's blue and something that's bluish?'

Taking it further

In conjunction with your thinking posters, have a thinking skills checklist in your classroom. Endeavour to practise every skill with the children as regularly as possible. Deliberately aim to build thinking into the curriculum.

Thinking time

"Early in my career, once I'd asked a question I couldn't stop myself jumping in quickly with the right answer if the children were silent."

Awareness of 'thinking time' will help children to become more effective and confident thinkers and forms a useful component of the pacing of your lessons.

The time you give the children to think should vary according to the kind of thinking you want them to do. Some basic principles for thinking:

- Value the children's thinking: This is perhaps the most important element of developing a 'thinking classroom'. It doesn't mean that you or the other children have to agree with what someone has said. But if a child has genuinely made an effort to think an idea through, then the effort itself can be praised even if the conclusion is erroneous.
- Make the thinking explicit: A child's verbal or written response will clue you in to how their minds work, thus you can infer or intuit the train of thought from what a child says. By feeding-back the thinking process, you not only give the child a chance to add to their ideas but also allow the whole class to become more familiar with a wide range of thinking techniques. So a typical response might be, 'So you thought about those three possibilities and decided that the third idea was the best one for reasons A, B and C...'
- Employ the principle of utilisation: Children are still learning (aren't we all!). The principle of utilisation advises that we take what the children offer and endeavour to respond to them in a way that helps them to learn and progress. So, instead of saying outright that an answer/idea is wrong, we could more usefully ask them to check again, or give it some more thinking time.

Teaching tip

Build thinking time into your lessons. For instance, if you're running a brainstorming session and you want quick-fire ideas, children will usually need some quiet time to figure out and consider alternatives. Offer thinking time and feel comfortable with the silence that follows.

I know this might sound stupid but...

"I used to say this all the time until I realised that my teacher really *did* want to know what I thought."

Developing effective and creative thinking goes hand in hand with allowing children to feel confident that their ideas are valued. However, this amounts to more than just saying 'I value your thinking': you have to demonstrate it.

Creativity is not a matter of 'anything goes'. Some ideas may well be 'silly' or not thought-out and some answers on matters of fact will certainly be wrong. Creating a thinking classroom requires teaching various thinking skills while encouraging the children to contribute their ideas. It's worth noting that 'en-courage' means 'to give one the courage'.

- Bear in mind the three-points rule: This well-known classroom ploy advises us to give three points of praise followed by one area for further thought/improvement. It works well when marking written work and can be adapted when children offer up ideas verbally. So you might say, 'I like the way you've thought that through, though you might want to check the conclusion.'
- Give sincere praise: Children soon see through the strategy of teachers tagging 'great, well done, brilliant' on to every idea they offer. Some ideas are none of these things, but if a child has tried the best then you can sincerely praise the effort (as psychologist Carol Dweck advises in her book *Self-Theories: Their Role in Motivation, Personality, and Development*).

How many uses for a paperclip?

"After we played this game we all agreed that paperclips were very useful indeed!"

This quick and easy activity encourages children to voice their ideas with confidence, creates an atmosphere where thinking is fun and reinforces the principle of 'How many ideas can we have and what use can we make of them?'

The value of this classic brainstorming game is that it is inclusive and there is no element of competition tempting more reticent children to have a go. The stages of brainstorming are:

- Clearly identify the concept to be explored or the problem to be solved.
- Ask for ideas off the top of the head.
- Record all ideas (using volunteer scribes or video).
- No ideas are to be commented upon (and certainly not judged) at this stage.
- Allow time for reflection, where children can refine, modify, prioritise ideas for usefulness and discard any that won't work.
- Allow time for groups to feed back their conclusions.

Ask the class to think of as many uses for a paperclip as they can. Specify a time limit of five minutes. Ideas are likely to come in a rush initially but may then start to thin out. You're looking for spontaneous thoughts so prompt and guide the children if they look as though they are 'trying hard to think' (otherwise known as 'head-scratching syndrome'). Try these ploys:

- Generalise ideas: If a child says, 'Earrings for a punk', you can prompt by saying, 'What other kinds of jewellery?'
- Jump to another point of view: For example, what use could Batman find for paperclips? What if paperclips were ten times bigger?

Teaching tip

Keep the game good-humoured. There is a definite link between laughter and good ideas!

Taking it further

Use brainstorming with other activities such as 'What if' (Idea 32) and 'Abandon Earth!' (Idea 90). You can also play the criss-cross game: What would you get if you crossed one or more paperclips with a Swiss army knife/a thermometer?

Dealing with feelings

"Being able to handle feelings more effectively goes hand in hand with developing thinking skills."

These related activities help children to become more emotionally resourceful. They also allow children to practise previously learned thinking skills while introducing them to some new ones.

Teaching tip

One teacher told his class that he would always be a 'caring presence' and that children could come and speak to him in confidence if they needed to. This kind of emotional support can be immensely helpful.

Taking it further

Another way of modifying feelings is the 'control panel' technique. Ask children to draw a control panel featuring buttons, dials or switches and then to decide what each of them controls. A 'happiness button' can be pressed on, an 'anger switch' switched off and so on. Drawing before and after versions of the panel will help to consolidate the work. With practice, most children can visualise their control panels and adjust the settings quickly and easily.

Develop emotional resourcefulness through these activities:

- Encourage children to notice feelings as they arise and to pinpoint their cause. Often our feelings 'go on in the background': for example, we might feel anxious but not consciously realise it, which makes resolving the matter much more difficult.
- Allow children to write about their emotions in a 'feelings journal'. Often writing about good feelings makes us stronger (especially if you read those entries again), while writing about bad feelings helps to 'get them off our chest'. Emphasise that the journals are private, but that if children want to talk about how they feel then that's fine.
- Anchor positive feelings (see Idea 50 'Anchor the learning') to create a link between a desired behaviour and something that is under your conscious control. Ask the class to remember a pleasant feeling – for example, happiness, a sense of achievement or confidence. As the children's feelings come forward, have them rub their thumb and little finger together (using the left hand for those that are right-handed, and vice versa).

This small, deliberate movement becomes associated in the mind with the positive feeling being remembered. Anchors develop over time so you'll need to run this activity regularly to maximise the effect. Once a child has established the anchor, when he next feels anxious, encourage him to do the little finger movement and this will help to diminish the unpleasant emotion by bringing the positive feelings to the fore. A really important aspect of emotional resourcefulness is to learn how to change a remembered viewpoint. Unpleasant experiences are usually remembered each time in the same way. By showing children how to change the way they remember unpleasant events, the negative emotional charge associated with them is usually diminished. This activity works best on a one-to-one basis, though you can also run it with a small group.

Explain to the children that you want them to remember a recent 'neutral' event – one that didn't elicit any particularly strong feelings. Using a neutral event familiarises children with the technique before they tackle unpleasant memories. Pleasant memories don't require changing: they do a good job being recalled just as they are!

As the children bring the memory forward, ask them to notice certain things about how they represent the experience in their imaginations. Are they seeing things through their own eyes or from a third person's perspective? Are they seeing images in colour or in black and white? Is there sound? Are any parts of the picture blurry? Are any parts particularly vivid? Get the children to notice if/how the memory changes their body posture and breathing.

Explain to the children that they are now going to run the memory again a number of times, each time changing one aspect of it. So if a child's memory was in colour, get them to make it black and white. If they remembered through their own eyes, get them to use his imagination to 'float up' and see the whole scene from above.

Ask the children to look at an interesting object in the room as they take a few deep breaths to bring them back to the present.

Bonus idea ★

A quick and effective technique for dealing with negative feelings is to imagine the feeling as a shape. Ask the child to tell you the shape of the feeling, its size, weight, colour, smell, texture, etc. Ask then where it is located inside the child. Now encourage the child to change every aspect of the object/feeling – work quickly through these and then ask the child to shift the feeling/object to some other part of the body before imagining they can remove it entirely and put it safely away in a box or a bag.

Note: You may think this sounds like a frivolous game, but because the mind and the body are linked what we think about and how we think has a powerful influence on our emotional landscape.

31

The world inside

"This game helps me to think of better characters for my stories. It also makes me realise that we all see things in different ways."

This activity develops the skills of noticing, associating and interpreting.

Show the class an image that depicts a variety of items such as peoples' faces, a distant building, an acorn, leaves or a computer (an example image of items can be downloaded from the online resources). Explain to them that the images are the thoughts going on inside a person's mind. Ask them, 'Why do you think he is thinking of these things? And why do you think he might be thinking of them *in this way*?' Point out that there's no single right answer to these questions. The aim of this task is to encourage children to make reasoned responses.

Below are some typical responses:

- 'I think it's autumn because of the acorns on the branch. I think this person is a boy who's not looking forward to going back to school.'
- 'I think this boy is clever because his brain is shining! But he feels nervous about working on computers.'
- 'On the right he's reaching for something...'
- 'Maybe something on a shelf? It's too high.'
- 'Or it could be he's worrying about reaching the next level in his SATs!'

Shoebox characters

"I've found that playing this game helps children to think outside the box."

Shoebox characters have applications in literacy and also help children to become familiar with inference, assumption and speculation.

Obtain some shoeboxes (or other boxes of roughly similar size or alternatively use jiffy bags) and either fill these yourself with a variety of small objects or ask the children to bring in items themselves. Each box is intended to contain actual objects/pictures of objects that a character owns, and which 'say something about' that character. If you ask children to create the boxes it is useful to have the groups think about what kind of character they want to focus on.

Once the boxes are completed, give one to each group (swapping boxes round if the children have made them) and set the task of making notes about the characters. Give some example descriptions of characters based on the contents, such as:

- 'There's a feeding bottle and baby wipes, so this character is likely to be someone with a baby.'
- 'There are train and aeroplane tickets in here, so this character probably likes travelling.'
- 'Here's a list of book titles so this person may like reading.'

Teaching tip

Emphasise words that suggest degrees of likelihood; for example, 'definitely', 'probably', 'likely', 'may', 'might', 'possibly'. Encourage children to choose these carefully. Also highlight 'reasoning words' such as 'because', 'so', 'therefore'. You can mention different kinds of thinking specifically, either before running the activity or during the feedback phase. You can find examples of thinking skills in Idea 99, 'Our amazing minds'.

Taking it further

Use this technique to help children 'flesh out' characters for their stories. Also, if you are studying a book with the class, ask what objects the different characters would put in their shoeboxes.

What if?

"Playing the 'what-if' game really helped me to learn about our topic of Africa and remember lots of facts."

'What if' is a versatile activity that can be used as a ten-minute brainstorm or as the basis for a much more extended topic.

Teaching tip

When you first run the activity make the question humorous and light-hearted. The fun element tempts more children to get involved, for example: 'What if people's thoughts appeared in thought bubbles above their heads and the colour of the bubbles reflected their mood?'

Taking it further

Select 'what ifs' as 'vehicles' for introducing ideas, facts and vocabulary relevant to a topic you want the class to study. For example, if you want to introduce the topic of Africa, ask: 'What if the Sahara desert suddenly started expanding, so that entire continent became a complete wilderness?'

Select an appropriate what-if topic and present it to the class. Some that I have found work well are:

- What if gravity switched off unexpectedly for ten minutes each day?
- What if, at age 50, people started to shrink, so that by age 75 they were only three inches tall?
- What if there was another intelligent species on Earth that was ten times more intelligent than humans?
- What if time moved at different rates on different continents?
- What if wishes came true just for one day?

Ask the children to discuss the 'what if' by focussing on these subsidiary questions:

- What would the world be like if...?
- What problems would there be if...?
- How could we solve those problems if...?

Even if the what-if question is impossible or fantastical the points it raises will often reflect back on real-world problems. The question about people shrinking, for instance, can lead to the class talking about equality in society and caring for older people, as well as raising thoughts about why creatures are the sizes they are, whether or not tiny humans really exist, plus more philosophical questions about age, what is life and why do we care for people?

Obserpinions

"When our teacher told us about this, I realised how much my thoughts and feelings are linked."

This activity develops reflectiveness and emotional resourcefulness. It also reduces the tendency for children to accept unexamined generalisations.

Explain that an 'obserpinion' happens when we react to something we've noticed without really thinking about it. In other words, the 'observation' and the 'opinion' are welded together so that the first impression triggers a knee-jerk reaction in terms of our emotional response.

There are two important points to make about this kind of thinking:

- Automatic emotional reactions are often 'picked up' from others; parents, peers, and so on, rather than being based on conclusions reached by the individual.
- If obserpinions are not examined, over time they can become generalisations that, though sometimes vague, carry a strong emotional charge. In other words, an individual can react out of all proportion to the observation that triggers the response.

After introducing the idea of obserpinions to the class, present them with a number of generalisations and ask children to rate how far they agree or disagree in each case:

- Tall people tend to live longer than short people.
- People who wear glasses are clever.
- Girls can't run as fast as boys. (This one usually gets a strong reaction!)
- You can't trust people who wear dark glasses on cloudy days.

Teaching tip

Revisit the activity a number of times. Encourage the children to take time to think, 'This is what I notice. This is how I feel about it – because...?'

Taking it further

Use the technique to help children understand: stereotyping in the media; emotive/persuasive language and rhetoric; how thinking of particular counter examples allows us to test generalisations; how our viewpoints can be conditioned by what other people think, and we don't always just make up our own minds.

But why?

"It feels great knowing I won't get told off for asking too many questions."

A key indicator of a successful thinking classroom is a decrease in 'reactive' thinking and an increase in proactive enquiry in the children.

Some children will take your permission to ask such questions as a licence to be silly or provocative. It is intensely irritating when a child says 'but why' to every statement you make. Lay down the ground rules at the outset. Like any technique, this one must be used appropriately by introducing the idea of relevance and appropriateness.

Thinking is 'reactive' when ideas and facts go unquestioned and unexplored by the children. It's true, of course, that some of the knowledge we offer has to be taken on trust: there simply isn't time to check everything, especially given the constant time pressure to cover the curriculum. However, when children passively accept facts as a matter of habit their learning is unlikely to develop far beyond the 'low order' thinking of recall and reiteration.

An environment where reactive thinking flourishes is characterised by the following indicators:

- The frequent asking of closed and/or rhetorical questions by the teacher.
- The simple restatement of facts by the children during the review phase of learning.
- 'Grasping and telling' behaviour, where children feel the need to hold on to 'right' answers and repeat them as a mark of achievement (often combined with a fear of being wrong).
- Children's heavy reliance on outside authority: unquestioned acceptance of received knowledge.
- A teaching/learning ethos that is overly judgemental, competitive and hierarchical (children always placed in rank order based on how much knowledge they remember).

Among the most powerful questions we can invite children to ask are:

But why? How do we know? Is that always true? What other examples of that are there? How can we check that? Where can I find out more?

Proactive thinking

"My experience has been that when children think more for themselves their enjoyment of learning increases and test results improve."

Curriculum content in the form of 'a body of knowledge' becomes more relevant and interesting to children when you encourage them to actively question the facts they must learn.

Children can soon be shown to take a more actively questioning approach as they learn. What's most important is their realisation that asking questions is not a sign of stupidity. I tell children that questioning is intelligent behaviour that says, 'I've identified something I don't understand and I'd like to learn more.'

A quick and effective way of highlighting proactive thinking is to write up on the board a supposed fact such as 'The Earth is round.' Do this before the children come into the room and notice how they respond. Ideally at least some of the children will ask the kinds of questions listed below. If no one reacts, kick-start the questioning process yourself.

- Why do you think the Earth is round?
- How can we check?
- What do we mean by 'round'? Is there a more accurate word or description we can use?

Eventually this kind of probing will lead to the kind of thinking behaviour you are looking for:

- Children will use the vocabulary of the subject more accurately and elegantly.
- They will generate more questions for themselves.
- They will become more inclined to find, check and elaborate upon answers for themselves.
- They will display the same behaviour across curriculum areas.

> **Teaching tip**
>
> For the questioning process, you can also ask deeper questions like, 'When do we know that something is a fact?', 'Can you think of any examples of an idea that wasn't a fact once but is now (or vice versa)?', 'Do you know of any facts that will always be true?'

Link up

"This deceptively simple activity really boosts children's creative thinking and makes them more confident."

One of the key elements of creative thinking is the ability to make meaningful connections between previously separate ideas.

Taking it further

Take the linking concepts the children suggest and ask for further examples. The linking concept behind Joseph's choice in the main idea is 'wood', so ask for more examples of wooden things. Ask if trees could fit into a bigger category than 'wood'. Someone is likely to suggest 'living things'. Invite further examples. You'll probably get both plants and animals. Ask what other categories these could fit into.

Bonus idea ★

Play 'guess the link'. Each day place two objects on the table and ask the children to suggest how they could be linked. Extend this by asking two children to bring in an object at random each day. How are they linked?

Show the class a picture of a selection of objects, for example, a mask, a watch, a key, cash, a pencil, sycamore seeds (an example picture of objects is available to download from the online resources.) Ask the children to pick any two items that are linked, for instance:

- Joseph: 'I pick the money and the pencil because they both come from trees. Paper is made from wood pulp – I don't mean that money grows on trees!'
- Caron: 'I pick the number and the money. If the number was the combination of a safe, the money could be kept in the safe.'
- Neil: 'I pick the digital player and the watch because they both have moving parts. Also, some digital players can also tell you the time.'

Add more objects to the selection and ask the class to link three objects. The items can be loosely themed or random, which adds to the challenge of creating links. Often, children will want to 'raise the bar' for themselves and will ask you if they can link four or more objects. This activity uses competitiveness as a positive force to test the children's thinking. Note: There is no one right answer to this task and it's not essential that every child take part: those who simply watch are still seeing how links can be made.

Category games

"The power of this game lies in asking children to think about *why* they put things into groups."

Categorising is a basic thinking skill that has applications in all subject areas. It is a flexible activity that you can tailor to the age/ability of your class and the topic you are working on.

Begin by listing ten items that you might find around the house (the children can suggest these). For example, cup, TV, saucepan, carpet, picture, chair, spoon, computer, soap, coffee. By definition they all fit into the category of 'household objects'. You can extend the activity in these ways:

- Are there two or more objects from the list that would fit into a different category? So TV and computer would fit into the category of 'electrical devices', cup and spoon would fit into 'kitchenware'. Think of other examples for each further category mentioned.
- Link the idea of categories by using sequencing. So using the household items above, ask the children to place them in order of size, cost, usefulness, etc. When differences of opinion crop up (as they are likely to!) encourage children to support their choices with reasons (using the sticky word 'because' – see Idea 2 'The mind is like...').
- Introduce or revisit Venn Diagrams when running category games. For example, TV and computer would fit into the overlapping circles of 'household objects' and 'electrical devices'. Could any further overlapping circles contain these two items? ('Modern inventions'? 'Educational tools'?)
- Ask the class to think of and research discoveries and inventions. Create a timeline display of these. Ask groups to add some interesting 'did you know' facts to each item.

Teaching tip

Categorising occurs across the subject range. For example, when children are familiar with the idea, use their experience to reinforce the notion of parts of speech. How would we define the category of verbs or adjectives? Do the same with number patterns. Explore how children categorise (label) themselves and others. How useful, valid or true are these categories?

Theme of the week

"Our teacher said that themes are 'big ideas' but that our imaginations are even bigger."

Themes are the solid platforms on which topics can be built. They also serve to connect different areas of the curriculum at a deep level.

Teaching tip

Pick out the themes of the children's favourite books and films. One way of helping children to identify themes is to ask, 'What is this story about?' Note that, most narratives have a primary theme, usually good versus evil, and that subsidiary themes are often built on this. Encourage children to think about themes as part of the planning of their own stories. Brainstorm plots around the chosen theme.

Teaching tip

Many questions in philosophy explore a number of basic themes, such as: morality, justice, freedom, reality, religion, love, thought, happiness, life and death, power, truth and belief. Consider how these could usefully form your theme of the week.

Take a theme such as 'identity'. First, ask the children what they understand by that word. Note down responses. Then split the class into groups and ask each group to create an association web around the concept (see Idea 6 'Word links, chains and webs'). Review the webs and help the children to create a workable definition of 'identity'. This idea can be extended into different subject areas:

- History/Geography: Can we say that the geographical features of a country contribute to its identity? What do we mean by 'cultural identity'? If I become a citizen of another country, will my identity change in any way? Can a period of time be said to have an identity – the Victorian era, for example, or the 1970s?
- Biology: Here we evoke the whole nature versus nurture debate. What are the links between our genes and our identities, 'who we think we are' as individuals?
- Philosophy: Ask 'what-if' questions around the theme. What if my mind could be transferred to someone else's brain? Would my identity disappear? Would I still be 'me'?

Playing with proverbs

"My made up proverb is 'A question a day keeps the boredom away!'"

These short, pithy sayings are a rich resource to encourage children to question, to increase their vocabulary and practise their inventiveness.

Using proverbs is an interesting way of encouraging children to think and to discuss their thoughts.

- Give the class a list of proverbs and discuss whether they are right or accurate and/ or where they would fit on a 1-6 scale of wisdom where 1 = not very wise and 6 = very wise. For instance, a class might think that 'Youth lives on hope, old age on remembrance' is wiser and more accurate than 'You can't teach an old dog new tricks'. If your children agree, ask them why they think it is wise or true/untrue.
- Ask the children to update old proverbs for the modern day. 'Stir up not the hornets' nest' becomes 'Don't disturb teachers in the staff room at coffee time.'
- Ask for possible explanations of obscure proverbs such as, 'Much cry, little wool.'
- Use proverbs as the basis for stories or other kinds of writing: 'There are none so blind as those who will not see.'
- Use proverbs for discussions/debates: 'The public pays with ingratitude.'
- Ask children to create short stories around 'pun-proverbs' such as, 'You can lead a hearse to water but you cannot make it sink.'

What kinds of questions?

"Our teacher thinks it's great when we ask questions. She says that asking a question we've thought about is a sign of curiosity and intelligence!"

Categorising questions helps children to understand how varied questions can be and also demonstrates the value and effectiveness of asking reasoned and relevant questions.

Begin by exploring the notion of questions generally. What kinds of questions can the children identify? Why ask questions at all? What questions are really important?

- Then place five or six shoeboxes on a table. Cut slots in the lids beforehand for the children to 'post' their questions later. Explain that questions come in all shapes and sizes. Give them an example, such as '3+3=?' Ask 'If we were going to put that question into one of the boxes, how could we label that box?' Each label is a category, for example: 'Easy questions'; 'Maths questions'; '"Small" questions'; 'Questions with one right answer'; 'Questions whose answers are facts not opinions'. If you have time, discuss with the class which label might be the most *useful* to put on the box.
- Show the class other types of questions to generate further categories. For example: What is the capital of England? Do you like apples? Are you truly happy? What is yellow? What is your favourite book?
- Allow the children time to talk about how they would categorise these questions. Then decide what labels to put on the boxes. Ask each child to write a question for as many categories as they can on scraps of paper and then to post them in the appropriate boxes.

Bonus idea ★

Ask the children to come up with the most interesting questions as possible in the following categories: Questions that have answers that are always right for everybody; Questions whose answers can change over time; Questions where someone's opinion would count as a 'right' answer; Questions that make you want to ask lots of other questions about the answer.

Questions audit

"Our teacher says that asking lots of good questions is like going on a learning quest."

Running a questions audit in your classroom, especially with the children's help, highlights the effectiveness of your strategy to build thinking skills into your teaching.

Essentially a questions audit checks the types and frequency of questions that you and the children ask during the course of a day. Some of the indicators of effective questioning in your classroom include:

- A balance between procedural questions and learning questions: Procedural questions are about the bare mechanics of the lesson, for example, 'Can I have a pen?' 'Can I go to the toilet?' 'Have you all got your books open on page 83?' Learning questions (from teacher or children) get to the solid content of the lesson. Learning questions seek clarification and further knowledge and also often help to generate further questions, for example, the open questions mentioned in Idea 34 'But why?'.
- Teacher-initiated and child-initiated questions: Questions asked by the teacher should be true to the meaning of the word education 'to draw out and rear up' (from the Latin). Some questions should be designed to find out how and to what extent children have understood a given set of ideas. This does not mean asking for the bland recall of facts, so where possible ask children to explain an idea in their own words.
- A good range of open questions: Where, what, what, who, why, how?
- Questions that you/the children ask about previous questions.

A cloud of questions

"At first it felt really strange asking so many questions. Even our teacher was joining in, and she told us she didn't know most of the answers."

The activity itself takes five to ten minutes but can lead to much more extensive pieces of work.

The immediate purpose of the activity is to shift the children's behaviour away from passive listening towards active questioning.

- Simply take an ordinary everyday object such as a coffee mug, show it to the class and tell them they (and you) have three minutes to compile as long a list – or 'cloud' – of questions as possible. Within the limits of good behaviour (!) all questions are admissible but must focus on – in this case – the coffee mug.
- If possible record all questions. Ask the children to make a note of the questions they asked. Alternatively video the session and enlist some friendly scribes to scribble them down.
- One benefit of 'a cloud of questions' is that it dampens the tendency for children to say 'I know this might sound stupid but...' since even the most apparently obvious, simple or naïve questions are acceptable, though sometimes these are deceptive – how many of us know why it's called a 'mug'? Or where the name 'coffee' comes from?

Bonus idea

Researching answers creates an enjoyable context for practising library and ICT skills.

Context sentences

"This is one of the best games I know for showing children how nosy human beings can be!"

This is a verbal and written variation of join-the-dots. We cannot help but see patterns and create contexts.

To get the game started, use a sentence such as: 'They shook hands, but only Baxter was smiling'. Note: A sentence like this is an example of so-called 'artful vagueness', where we are given some precise information that also begs many questions.

Show the sentence to the children. Their first task is to notice what they are imagining as they read it (see Ideas 8, 12-20). Either go round the class to collect opinions or ask the children to make notes on what they 'see'.

Now split the class into small groups and ask each group to think of up to ten questions they could ask about the sentence. Using a question star (see Idea 42 'A cloud of questions') is a useful prompt to give the children focus. Then harvest some questions and put them up on the board according the four main elements of mind mapping, as follows:

1 Put different categories of question in different areas of the visual field.
2 Colour-code the different kinds of questions (for example, 'where' questions in red, 'when' questions in orange).
3 Highlight key words.
4 Invite logical or reasonable connections between different categories of question. For example, can children think of a reasonable link between why the characters were shaking hands and what else might be happening?

Taking it further

Use the children's responses to highlight the thinking skills of speculation and assumption. How many of the children assumed that Baxter was a man?

'Toggle' between open questions and closed questions. Turn 'What was Baxter wearing?' into a number of closed questions (for example, 'Was Baxter wearing a suit?') and use the coin flip technique to gather information (see Idea 76 'Flip it').

Use context sentences as a basis for planning stories. Ask the children to make up their own examples.

Twenty questions

"This game is much more than a time filler. It really gets children thinking about the quality of their questions."

One game of 'twenty questions' takes between five to ten minutes, though you can extend the activity to explore notions of relevance and incisiveness, two key criteria for asking quality questions.

Most children will already be familiar with the game of twenty questions.

- Show the class a grid (an example grid is available to download from the online resources) and ask one of the children to select an item, for example, an animal, and write its name down on a scrap of paper, which she then hands to you (so that you can prompt and guide as necessary).
- The other children are invited to ask questions to try and work out which animal has been picked.
- Do not allow blind guesses. If a child thinks she knows what the animal is, she must summarise the evidence/clues she has gathered to inform her answer: in other words, ask for a chain of reasoning.
- The child who gives the right answer is now allowed to choose the next item (in this case an animal) and the game continues.

Taking it further

Add an element of competitiveness by splitting the class into groups and awarding points. If someone gives a right answer after one question, they earn 20 points. If they give a right answer after two questions, earn 19 points, etc. Points can also be awarded when children correctly use relevant vocabulary in their questions.

Use theme grids (for example, the genre grid in Idea 79) according to the topic, subject area or class reader you're currently studying. Ask groups to make up grids of their own.

Bonus idea

Use a word grid instead of a picture grid. Encourage children to use the vocabulary of literacy – noun, apostrophe, syllables, etc.

Pretend we know nothing

"This game had a lot of us giggling, and it felt great that for once we didn't have to remember things we'd been taught."

The activity combines 'A cloud of questions' (Idea 42) and association webs (see Idea 6) with information retrieval/research skills.

Ask the children to focus on something in the classroom and pretend they know nothing about it. Whereas in Idea 42, 'A cloud of questions', the aim was to brainstorm as many questions as possible in a given time, here the emphasis is on trying to find answers as you go along and using questions to generate further questions and lines of enquiry.

For example, if you focussed on the window, the activity might run like this:

- Primary question: 'I wonder why it's called a window?'
- Secondary questions: 'Could it have something to do with the phrase "a window of opportunity"?'; 'Are flat sheets of glass always called panes?' 'Where does the word "pane" come from?'
- Primary question: 'How is glass made?'
- Secondary questions: 'Does anything like glass occur naturally?'; 'Are all windows made of glass?'; 'How many kinds of glass are there?'; 'Is the glass in my spectacles the same stuff as window glass?'

Teaching tip

For certain questions, give the class several possible answers and ask them to work out which they think is the right/most likely answer and why.

Taking it further

Split the class into small research teams. Each team must find out some facts about the object or topic in question and offer a short five minute, informative presentation to the rest of the class. Encourage a variety of presentations (for example, talk, slide show, piece of drama, artwork).

The three-step technique

"This is a very effective strategy for developing what I call power questioning."

Once children have learned this very easy technique they can apply it to many areas of their learning.

The three-step questioning technique is to ask:

1 What do we know?
2 What do we think we know?
3 What do we need to ask to find out more/to be sure?

The first question focuses attention on what can be directly observed and on matters of fact. The second question highlights speculations, assumptions and inferences. The third question demands the framing of relevant and incisive lines of enquiry. We can use the following extract to illustrate the three-step questioning technique:

> 'It was one of those slightly misty evenings when the chilly air seemed to me to smell of smoky metal. Above a thin ground mist a few stars gleamed faintly in the sky. Even though November 5th was still two days away, somebody was letting off fireworks in one of the back gardens along Wyland Park Road behind the supermarket.'

Some of the things *we know are*: the date is November 3rd; it's dark and cold; at least one person is present (the narrator). *What we think we know* includes: Where the narrator is standing is not very far from where the fireworks are being let off (because otherwise he or she would not be able to hear or see them). The location is probably a town (because you're less likely to find a supermarket in a village. If this were a city, would you be able to see stars even on a fairly clear night?).

Taking it further

Consider practising the three-step technique further by using a picture (as in Idea 13 'First impressions') and a set of clues (as in Idea 56 'The detective game').

The computer in the box

"I like this game – but it would be great if a computer really could answer our questions!"

This activity takes a minimum of 20 minutes and helps children to prioritise questions in terms of relevance, robustness and information-gathering power.

Put a tablet or laptop-sized package on the table and explain to the class that inside is a super-intelligent computer that can answer any question. Ask the children to write down four or five questions (on their own or in small groups) they would really like to know the answers to.

- Now explain that the computer is a bit like a grumpy professor and doesn't have the patience to answer questions that the children already know the answers to. Ask the groups to strike out any questions of that kind.
- Explain now that the computer is not like a human: it can only process questions that are absolutely clear and unambiguous. For example, if one question is, 'How can I grow rich?' the computer would ask what are the meanings of the words 'grow' and 'rich'. Ask the children to redraft their questions as necessary.
- Each child/group should now have a shortlist of high-quality questions. Put these up on the board. If there are too many you can either ask children to pick their individual favourite, or go through the weeding process several times.
- Now explain that because the computer uses a lot of energy it only has enough battery power to answer three questions. The task for the children is to discuss and decide which three questions to ask.

Teaching tip

Some children feel on safer ground if they ask a question to which they already know the answer. One of the aims of this activity is to allow children to learn that uncertainty, ambiguity and simply not knowing are important aspects of their learning

Taking it further

Focus the question selection on a current topic or area of study. Play 'letter to an expert', where the children create three questions to ask an expert (alive or dead) on a chosen subject. If you could ask an author three questions about his/her book, what would they be?

The VERV strategy

"This activity helped us to understand that behind every good idea there is a lot of hard work."

The VERV strategy can be built into any project that leads children from first idea to finished product.

Teaching tip

Enthusiasm is infectious. You can help to charge up the positive emotional energy in the classroom through your own enthusiasm. Initially talking about a favourite book, film or hobby sets the tone. Give children the chance to talk about their own interests and pastimes. Use techniques like anchoring (See Idea 50) or control panel (See Idea 29) to help children access the feeling of enthusiasm whenever they need to.

The immediate aim of this strategy is to provide a structure for thinking; to give a sense of direction in clarifying ideas and turning them into desired outcomes. VERV combines emotional resourcefulness with thinking skills.

- **V**ision: This has also been called the 'Dreamer' phase, where children can enjoy letting their ideas flow. It's important that ideas are not analysed or judged at this point; rather it is a question of how many ideas can be generated – the notion of 'What use can we make of these ideas?' comes later. Brainstorming is a useful precursor to successfully developing a vision.
- **E**nthuse: Enthusiasm is the emotional energy that drives the project, that brilliant sense of excitement, playfulness, curiosity and optimism that powers us on to achieve.
- **R**ealise: This means to 'make real' in your life; to consciously recognise and understand an idea so that it can be thought about and acted upon, to see something actually come to fruition. This is where the balance shifts towards more critical/analytical kinds of thinking (though still buoyed up by the energy of enthusiasm).
- **V**erify: This involves looking back or checking to see if a plan has worked or if more needs to be done. It is also the 'What have I learned?' stage of the project, which will make the next one even more successful.

Taking it further

You can build VERV into small-scale projects like a piece of writing, or something much bigger like a school play, a day trip, a residential course, etc. VERV projects can also be hypothetical as in 'Abandon Earth!' (Idea 90).

Watch your language

"Language is the most powerful teaching tool that we have. Every word matters."

Language awareness generates many activities but more importantly contributes to our attitude when it comes to classroom interactions.

Language frames our reality. The way we explain our understanding of the world influences how we and our children react to it. This insight allows us to use language much more effectively in helping children to learn.

Look out for these and similar limiting patterns in children's language:

- Unhelpful metaphors: 'It's an uphill struggle'; 'I've hit a brick wall'; 'I can't get my head around this'; 'I'm stuck'; 'It's no use'; 'It's (or I'm) hopeless'. Intervening is not so much a matter of stopping children from speaking in this way, but helping them to recognise the metaphor and use it more positively. If something is an uphill struggle, what a view you'll get when you reach the top! If there's a brick wall in your way, let's see what the bricks (component parts) actually are and dismantle them one at a time. One of the most inhibiting metaphors I've found is 'writer's block'. Why not call it 'writer's opportunity' or 'writer's playground'? If you call it a 'block' it will do just that: block.
- All or nothing thinking: Look out for 'never' and 'always': 'I never get this right'; 'I'm always getting into trouble'. Remind the child of times when this was not the case.
- Labelling: A label turns a process into a state. Look out for children labelling themselves – thick, slow, dull, etc. Again, endeavour to redress the balance with counter examples.

Teaching tip

Be aware of more general metaphors in education: keeping up, slipping back, falling behind, stretching, pulling, pushing and even drilling. This is the language of the 'rat race', which can even become militaristic when we begin talking of targets or describing people as 'cohorts' – a word originally used to describe groups of Roman soldiers and not an accurate term to describe people today!

Anchor the learning

"Anchoring is one of the most effective techniques I know for classroom management and a great way to focus children's attention and thinking."

An 'anchor' is used in this sense to describe a link that you create between a certain behaviour you want from the children and a 'trigger' that is under your control.

Anchoring is a cumulative technique that gradually gives children more choice and control over the kinds of thinking they can do.

- Decide on several useful behaviours you want the children to improve on. Examples of behaviours you might choose include: paying attention, thinking about new ideas, asking relevant questions, making creative connections, reviewing and revising previous work, and so on.
- Now choose several specific spots in the classroom where you will stand when you want the children to behave in these ways. You can associate several behaviours with one spot.
- Get into the habit of moving to the designated spot when you want the children to do the behaviour associated with it. Don't be obvious about it and don't tell the children what you're doing. Anchoring is a 'subliminal' technique: the children will create the association between spot and behaviour at a subconscious level. However, you should be explicit about the behaviours themselves. For example, you can place yourself at the 'paying attention' spot and say, 'OK, today we're going to begin a new topic. I'd like you to pay attention and think about what I tell you.'

As a matter of fact

"Increasingly I say to the children, 'What's the best question you've asked today?'"

The factual content of the curriculum is the raw material that we use to develop children's thinking, but this raw content must be connected, turning it into ideas that children can challenge and learn from.

Here are some questioning strategies you can teach to help children turn 'content' into information and ideas.

- Precise questioning. Questions like these ask for further, clearer details or explanations. 'What exactly do you mean by...?'; 'How specifically does that happen?'; 'Can you explain further...?'; 'How precisely did people find that out...?'
- Assess the information in terms of:
  - How recent it is. (Has it been superseded?)
  - How 'universal' it is. (Is it always the case/always true?)
  - Where it comes from. (Check more than one source for accuracy.)
  - How it is presented. (Does the presentation aid understanding?)
  - Whether or how fact is mixed with opinion. (Personal opinion or general bias?)
  - Whether the author is trying to persuade or be unbiased. (Look out for emotive language/lack thereof?)
  - Whether examples support general statements. (Look also for counter examples.)
- There will never be time to help children question all of the information we present to them, but if we want them to develop as independent, creative thinking adults we must sometimes give them the opportunity to challenge the facts we deliver.

Be reasonable

"Miss Madigan told us that the word 'reason' means to think and 'to make fit'. That helped me when I had a quarrel with Linda!"

The notion of 'reasons' can be used as the basis for a variety of lessons across a range of subject areas.

The educationalist John Abbott maintains that young children especially have the wonderful ability to create 'naïve theories of everything'. As we grow older, our theories of how the world works become more sophisticated and informed, although there is a danger that we can become unquestioningly dogmatic in our views. Here are a few ideas on how to incorporate 'reasons' in your lessons:

- Ask children to explain different phenomena. Their explanations can be weird and wonderful. Questions to ask include: 'Why does the sun rise and set?'; 'What is thunder?'; 'Why can't you ever find the end of a rainbow?'
- Story planning: Explain that, generally, in good stories everything happens for a reason and that this helps the story to be better. This applies at the more general level of character motivation, but also comes down to the choice of words and phrases.
- Rewrite a short extract from a story deliberately choosing less powerful or elegant words – in other words, make the extract less well written! Now ask the children to suggest improvements and explain why they are necessary.
- Discuss character motivation. Why does a certain character act in a particular way? Are there clues in the narrative or do we have to speculate?
- Look at poetry and discuss why the writer might have set it out as she did.

The strength of reasons

"This activity develops reflectiveness and allows children to realise the importance of supporting their opinions and arguments with reasons."

This activity can be used as a five-minute lesson starter or form the basis of a more extended project.

Begin by presenting the class with a situation and a list of reasons that may explain it. Ask the children to decide which reason is the strongest or most convincing and why. Discuss how the reasons might be put in rank order from strongest to weakest, encouraging the children to justify their choices. For example:

Situation

'I was walking home from school when I found a purse in the street. There was £50 inside and I decided to keep it because...'

Reasons
- 'Any normal person would do the same.'
- 'Our family is poor and we really need the money.'
- 'I've spent all of my pocket money.'
- 'I wanted to buy my best friend a present for her birthday.'
- 'If people are that careless with their money they deserve to lose it!'
- 'The purse was made of expensive leather so the owner must be rich and can afford to lose £50.'
- 'I wanted to donate the money to a local charity.'
- 'My gran needs an operation and I can put the money towards her having it done privately.'

Taking it further

Make a slight change to one or more of the reasons and ask the children if they think that makes it more convincing, less convincing, or leaves it unchanged in the ranking. For example, 'I wanted to buy my best friend a present for her birthday. She's very ill in hospital at the moment.'

Pyramid planning

"I like the pyramid idea because I can imagine the shape easily whenever I want to."

This planning template can be used for children's narrative and non-fictional writing and also to develop their thinking skills.

The pyramid shape is a visual analogue that connects the general to the particular. It also emphasises 'layeredness' in terms of text, for example, the structure of a story or a newspaper report, where each layer builds on the one before, working up to the top. Children can use pyramids in their written work by dividing a pyramid into the required number of layers/sections and making brief notes in each as they think about their project. This technique helps children to gain an overview of the work (in creative writing, for example, linking broad themes to the actions and dialogue of the characters – see below) while also giving them a step-by-step approach towards a finished product. Here are some examples of how pyramids are seen in text:

- Pyramids are vital in story planning. From the bottom up, they include: Narrative elements (hero, villain, problem, journey, partner, object). Themes (the main ideas behind the story). Genre (fantasy, horror, romance). Motifs (these can be characters, scenes, dialogue, objects or set pieces of action that help to define and describe the genre).

- Pyramids can be seen in newspaper articles. From the top down: Headline – byline (one or two sentences summing up the nature of the article) – key ideas (a paragraph giving the main gist of the story) – development (a sequence of paragraphs that expand on the key ideas) – quotes and opinions – conclusion or rounding off.

Taking it further

The pyramid can even be used to explain the three-step questioning technique (Idea 46, 'The three-step technique'). From the top down: What do I know? – What do I think I know? – What questions must I ask to find out more/be sure?

Points of view

"To get to know someone, walk a mile in his shoes."

Being able to see things from a different point of view is an important thinking skill that has many applications.

Try the following activities to illustrate different viewpoints to the children:

- Play the 'while' game. Begin with a simple sentence such as: 'Jones lay slumped on the sofa.' Then say, '*While* Jones lay slumped on the sofa, in the flat next door...' and ask for a suggestion. If a child says, 'The neighbours were quarrelling,' then you say, 'While the quarrel was going on, in the street outside...' And ask for another idea, moving further away from Jones each time. This activity helps children to develop an overview of what is happening. After the game, draw concentric circles on the board. Each circle represents a stage of the game. Jones goes in the small central circle, the quarrel in the next circle out and so on. The children copy the diagram and add further ideas to each circle.
- After studying a class reader, ask the children to pick a character and rewrite a scene from that person's point of view.
- When staging a debate, ask the children to write down which side they're on and why, then ask them to argue *from the opposite point of view*.
- Play 'decision alley'. Decide on an issue and clarify points for and against. Split the class into two groups and form two lines facing each other. Each line represents one side of an argument. Invite other students to walk down the decision alley while your class (in a polite, controlled way) reiterate the points of the argument.

The detective game

"This game really helps me to be nosy – to notice, ask questions and think."

This basic activity takes about ten minutes and consolidates a number of the techniques found elsewhere in this book.

Put a series of clues on the board that suggest (but do not specify) an everyday event. For example:

- The fanlight window in the kitchen is open.
- The teacloth that was covering the plate on the worktop is now on the floor.
- There is no food on the plate.
- There are grease marks on the worktop near the plate.
- The cat does not appear when she is called.

Ask the children to suggest the most likely thing to have happened. Most will probably say that the cat came in smelling food, she hooked the teacloth off the plate to get to the meat underneath, ate the meat then climbed through the fanlight window to escape.

Next draw a line on the board and mark it 1-6. Tell the class that the cat story ranks as a '1' on the line because it is an ordinary event that is likely to happen. Ask for ideas that would be '2' on the line – incidents that would be a little more unusual. Every few minutes, ask the children to move another notch along the line, inventing ever more weird and wonderful stories as they go. Bring in genre. Say, 'Who can make up a story that is a 3 on the line and a Romance?'

Ideas matrix

"When the mind is thinking, it is talking to itself." Plato

This basic activity focuses on an aspect of thinking called 'chunk size', which is our potential to think both in vague generalised terms – 'big chunk ideas' – and of particular details – 'small chunk thoughts'.

On the board, draw two lines to form a right angle, positioning the angle towards the bottom left. Label the vertical axis 'small-big' and the horizontal axis 'particular-general'. For example, a small, particular idea or a fact would go near the bottom left. Now discuss with the class whereabouts on the matrix the following ideas would fit:

- Put a raw egg still in its shell into water. If it floats it means it's gone off.
- 12 x 12=144.
- Time.
- The number 64 bus goes to the centre of town.
- French people.
- There are both African elephants and Indian elephants.
- The name of a person.

Teaching tip

Introduce or revise co-ordinates. Ask the children to draw the matrix on squared paper with the axes A-Z and 1-26. Ask each child to choose a colour and to colour in one of the squares without showing anyone else. Go around the class asking the children to give the colour and position of their chosen square, which their classmates now colour in.

Taking it further

Play 'lift the stone'. Write down six sets of co-ordinates according to a pattern – for example, A1, B2, C3, etc. Tell the class to imagine that each square of the matrix is covered by a stone and that six treasures are hidden under six stones. Tell the class where to find the first treasure and that they must spot the pattern for finding the others. Each time a child or group gives you a set of co-ordinates you tell them whether they have found a treasure or not. The first group to work out the pattern wins the round.

Link to think

"Making links and looking at things in different ways are the foundations of thinking."

Any activity that encourages children to make mental links strengthens their ability to think both creatively and analytically.

Here are some activities to help children to start making links:

- Split the class into groups and give each group a large sheet of paper. Ask every group to write the same word, for example, 'blue', in the middle of the sheet and four other words, any words, in the four corners; for example, 'sun', 'concrete', 'aunt', 'time'. The children must create a reasonable chain of ideas linking 'blue' with each of the other words. The first one is relatively easy – blue-sky-sun. The last, where an abstract concept is the end point, is harder – blue-mood-boredom-endless-time. Challenge the groups further by seeing if they can create association chains connecting the corner words.
- Use word association as a planning tool for characters and plots in stories. Ask the children to free-associate around a character's name, an object, an incident and then use some of these connections to create a more linear narrative.
- Show the class partial patterns or sequences of numbers or letters and ask the children to work out how the sequence continues.
- Use grading exercises as a 'mind warm-up' at the start of a lesson. For example, write the names of cities on the board and ask children to work out their progressive distance from your school.
- Look at advertising to see how language is linked to target audiences.

Seed thoughts

"If the logical conscious mind was the size of my hand, the creative subconscious would be the size of my classroom."

Creative thinking sometimes happens most effectively by letting ideas grow by themselves, 'in the back of the mind'.

Here are a few techniques for exploiting the creative subconscious:

- Introduce the class to 'seed thoughts'. These are small prompts around which larger ideas grow. They can take the form of an object, words or a picture and act as a stimulus for further unanticipated connections to be made. For example, show the class an egg timer and explain that this will give the children ideas for a story that you want them to write tomorrow. Suggest that when you eventually remind them of the egg timer they'll know *much more* about how it fits into the story. Show the class the egg timer again next day and ask the children to jot down any ideas that drift into their heads.
- Get your class to use systematic daydreaming (as opposed to idle daydreaming!). Decide first on the purpose for the daydreaming – ideas for a story, solving a problem or revising a topic. Then make a list of ten or so words to act as prompts. Ask the children to settle themselves and take a few slow deep breaths. Now begin to read from the list, one word at a time with a pause of ten to 15 seconds between each (if revising you can take key words from an association web that the children can also glance at). After the last word has been read, ask the children to (quietly) jot down their thoughts.

Teaching tip

For 'seed thoughts', a clear intention that the technique will work is important. 'When' is a powerful prompt to get results; it acts as a presupposition of success, so that subconsciously the children will register and react to your suggestion that ideas appear.

The maybe hand

"The maybe hand lets me have five ideas or more without worrying about which one is right."

This simple technique allows children to understand in a visual and tactile way the mental structure of speculation.

If you have used Idea 13 'First impressions', where the children speculate about a particular scene, it's likely a few of the children will have used the word 'maybe' already: 'Maybe he's [the man walking down the alley] a thief'; 'Maybe people are chasing him'; 'Maybe he has jewels in the bag'.

- Formalise the children's speculations by getting them to hold out a hand, palm upwards. You should model this first. Tell them to imagine that the subject of the image they are speculating about is in the middle of the palm, for example, who the man might be. Then say, 'OK, so maybe he is a thief...' Touch your thumb to indicate that idea. Then touch your index finger. 'Or maybe he's (a)...?'

- Any child can offer another idea: speculation is about having lots of ideas at this stage rather than judging any of them as correct/incorrect. Once children understand this, further ideas will come along – you may need to use both of your hands (and perhaps one or two of the children's!). When you have at least one handful of ideas say, 'Now look what we've got, a handful of treasures to think about later.'

- This technique trains children to have ideas in multiples rather than singly. The palm of the hand acts as the focus for the thinking while the thumb and fingers represent five possible explanations to be investigated later.

Taking it further

Transfer the skill to other subjects. Set up an experiment such as placing sugar crystals in hot water. Say, 'Using the maybe hand, what do you think might affect what happens to the crystals?' For example: Maybe... the temperature of the water; Maybe...the size of the crystals; Maybe... movement in the water; Maybe...the length of time the crystals are in the water; Maybe...other liquids or objects put in the water.

The why game

"When children start asking *why* for themselves, I know that my thinking skills agenda is working."

Asking 'why' is a matter of confidence.

Children need to feel confident that they will not be negatively judged or thought 'stupid' by not already knowing the answer, and we need to feel comfortable saying, 'I don't know, but how could we find out?' That said, children need to be shown how to ask 'why' appropriately. Emphasise from the outset that 'silly' kinds of behaviour are unacceptable and that questions need to be relevant and appropriate.

Deliberately set up learning situations that encourage children to ask why, such as:

- When studying a novel, bring up the idea of the author's intention. Why did he choose that word, this metaphor? Why did the character do A and not B?
- Look at how magazines and non-fiction books are designed. Why are the pictures that size? Why did the editor choose those colours for the headings?
- In Science, rather than just telling the children the facts all of the time, every now and then take the opportunity to show them the experiment or explain the phenomenon and then ask them to speculate as to possible explanations.
- Set why-type questions as research tasks: Why do other primates have more hair than humans? Why is London the capital of England? Why is the Sahara desert spreading? Why do cats have whiskers? Why did the Romans build such straight roads?

> **Teaching tip**
>
> Use this activity as an opportunity to demonstrate to children that some questions have one right answer, some have many acceptable answers, some probably have answers but we haven't found/don't know them yet, and some questions may be inherently unanswerable.

Personifying

"This thinking skill helps children to gain real insight into abstract concepts."

'Personifying' is the imaginative ability we have to invest objects, ideas and feelings with human qualities; or by a leap of the imagination to identify with objects — to 'become' it so that we can see the world from another point of view.

Personification can benefit children who like to learn in a more tactile way (the more kinaesthetically-oriented thinkers — see Idea 17 'Jump in'). I once observed a science lesson where the children were taken to the hall and encouraged to dance in groups holding hands as they imagined they were starch molecules. Other classmates came along and broke the groups apart. They were enzymes. Just watching the lesson was memorable: I haven't forgotten it to this day and daresay the children who took part in the lesson haven't either.

Here are a few suggestions for you to incorporate personification into your lessons:

- Take an emotion such as apprehension. If 'apprehension' were a person, what would they look like? If a feeling were to become an animal, what would the animal look like? How would it behave?
- Work with the children to personify different natural phenomena, such as: the rain cycle, the Moon orbiting the Earth, orbiting the Sun, or the evolution of simple life forms into more complex creatures.
- Model the idea by personifying different substances, such as: diamonds, fire, water and wood. Speak and act as though you were that thing. What are your strengths and weaknesses? What does the world look like to you? How do you react with other substances and forces?

Taking it further

Read some myths and legends with the class and point out that the various gods and goddesses were often personifications of natural processes and also human qualities (for example, the fact that the god of Mars represented war). Ask the children to find images of these gods and explain in more detail how their appearance is connected with the thing they personify.

Solve it

"We cannot solve our problems with the same thinking we used to create them." Albert Einstein

Problem-solving tasks help to consolidate a range of thinking skills and combine the creative and critical abilities of the mind. They also support collaborative learning, help to develop children's confidence and cultivate a 'can do' attitude.

Here is a general strategy when setting up problem-solving activities:

1 Define the problem clearly. Break it down into smaller parts that can be worked on separately if possible.
2 Imagine outcomes. What will a successful result look like and feel like?
3 Be goal-oriented. Maintain a clear intention that the problem will be successfully tackled.
4 Think strategically. Consider a number of routes towards solving the problem. That sometimes means thinking 'off the wall'.
5 Notice your own thoughts: inklings, insights, intuitions. Sometimes the smallest, fleeting thought can lead to success.
6 Apply the VERV model – see Idea 48.

Below are some tasks for the children to tackle. Split the class into groups and ask them to apply the problem-solving strategy to work towards a solution. Point out that there may be several workable solutions to each problem:

- A supermarket chain wants to boost its sales by 10% this year. How can you help?
- The local police force in your area wants to reduce burglaries. What do you suggest?
- The school librarian wants to make the library more popular. How can this be achieved?
- My cat keeps scratching at the furniture. I don't want to get rid of it, what shall I do?

Taking it further

Combine the problem-solving strategy with the mysteries technique (See Idea 89). Ask the children to assemble information on scraps of paper and rearrange and reorganise these as a way of approaching a solution.

Thinking about thinking

"I never realised how many different kinds of thinking I can do."

An important aspect of developing thinking skills is to reflect on the thinking process itself. Using metaphors gives children a deeper understanding of the versatile processes of thought.

Many schools are now familiar with Edward de Bono's idea of the Six Thinking Hats: information, thinking about thinking, judgement, feelings, creativity, benefits. This model highlights the vital insight that the mind is capable of a variety of ways of thinking and that thoughts are linked to brain states and are influenced by feelings.

We have looked at types of thought elsewhere in this book, for example, we looked at metacognition, one's ability to notice and manipulate thoughts in Idea 8 'Notice your thoughts'. We've also seen how metaphors offer a powerful way of helping us to think effectively in Idea 2 'The mind is like...' and Idea 49 'Watch your language'.

You can help children to become more aware of how their minds are working by creating names for the different ways they think and how this relates to their feelings. For instance, sometimes children's minds can't focus on a task but seem to flit from idea to idea almost randomly. Calling this 'butterfly thinking' is more useful than recognising the child is finding it hard to pay attention. It also helps the child to identify and recognise that kind of thinking, while the metaphor can be exploited more positively: butterflies are also capable of sitting still with wings open, soaking up the sun. If the child realises her mind is 'fluttering' ask her to settle to butterfly on a 'sunny wall' and notice what that *feels* like.

Taking it further

What other kinds of thinking can the children identify? How does it help to call problem solving 'jigsaw puzzle thinking'? What metaphor could we pin to speculation? How might 'Velcro thinking' work? (Velcro thinking is a strategy where ideas can be linked but also easily separated and rearranged.) If a child is worried, what metaphor could we come up with to lessen that child's anxieties?

Attributing

"Sometimes it's scary to realise how we don't 'make up our minds' at all, but they are actually made up for us!"

An attribute is a characteristic or quality we associate with a person, creature, place or object. 'Attributing' is the process of linking qualities and traits to things.

Ideally attributing should be done consciously and deliberately, but often people accept and react to 'pre-packaged' sets of attributes without reflecting on them.

- Introduce attributing as a thinking skill by showing the class a familiar object, say a pencil. Ask the children to help you list its characteristics and features – thinking of simple adjectives is a great way to start (long, thin, wooden, ordinary, useful).
- Discuss the attributes necessary for different jobs or endeavours. For instance, ask what attributes are necessary to be a successful athlete, doctor, farmer or teacher.
- Link attributes with stereotyping. Show the children pictures of different stock characters, for example, from movies or comics. What are the children's immediate reactions? Now tease out the observed attributes of these characters and reflect how easy it is to have a 'knee-jerk' response.
- Use attributing to assess the relative strengths and weaknesses of things. For instance, what are the attributes of a paperback book and an e-reader? Which attributes of each do the children think are advantages and weaknesses?

Teaching tip

When the children are learning to see attributing as a thinking skill, point out that what the children are doing is not the same as associating (see Idea 6 'Word links, chains and webs'). I can associate the pencil with the time when Jamie scribbled all over my book, but the scribbling is not an attribute of the pencil itself.

Taking it further

Give the class a list of attributes for the line 'My cat Scamp'. Ask them to rearrange the words in order of the smallest/most individual attributes to the most general characteristics. So the solution to the task is: Scamp, tabby, cat, domestic pet, feline, mammal, animal, living organism. This activity also leads in to the process of classifying, in this case of animals.

Coat of arms

"Mr Buck let me put *'Semper arridente'* on my coat of arms. It means 'Always smiling'!"

Devising a personal coat of arms allows children to reflect on their positive attributes: it also helps them to clarify their intentions, celebrate their achievements and acts as a powerful visual reminder of their qualities, beliefs and values.

Begin by looking at the emblems for your own school and others (keying 'school emblems' into Google will return scores of examples). Discuss what the various aspects and their positioning on the emblem could mean. Note that you are asking the children to speculate or infer at the moment. Time permitting, show the children some traditional heraldic symbols and how these represent qualities, beliefs and values.

- Ask the children to think about their own personal qualities. Point out that listing these is not showing off, but is more a matter of self-esteem and self-respect. For instance, if I am a patient person, that is something to be pleased about.
- Now ask the children what objects, animals or plants represent their qualities. Ask them to think about the overall shape or template for their coat of arms. What would a shield shape suggest or represent? What does a circle or star shape say about the person?
- Let the children draw the motifs on their coat of arms (clipart for these is readily available). Finally ask each child to think of a motto that sums up a significant quality – this can be written in any language, though Latin does sound grand!

Similar and different

"My friend Naseem said we are all in the same boat together but there is no one else like me, so we are both right."

Comparing and contrasting combines a number of other thinking skills including associating, attributing, classifying and generalising.

Comparing and contrasting is a wonderfully versatile strategy that is simple when you introduce it to younger children but becomes much more sophisticated and challenging for older thinkers and incorporates other key thinking skills.

- A basic activity is to show the children two animals such as a cat and a dog. Ask in what ways they are similar, then discuss the differences. Even at this elementary level you can introduce some more technical vocabulary to do with the classification of animals (such as: vertebrate/invertebrate, reptile/mammal, canine/feline).
- Increase the number of objects to compare and contrast. For example, show the children a selection of leaves. Ask how we know that they are all leaves – what are their attributes? Now investigate differences in terms of size, shape, colour and texture. Note that these categories can be applied to other selections of objects.
- Focus on feelings. How are happiness and joy similar? What differences between these emotions can children pinpoint?
- Use similes to pinpoint the common attributes of different things. For example: As red as...? As agile as...? As industrious as...?
- Ask the children to find a partner and compare and contrast themselves in a positive way. Use this activity as the basis for discussing individuality and uniqueness.

Taking it further

Link the idea of similarities and differences with the activity of 'Would you rather...?' Ask the children, for example, 'Would you rather be a bird or a cloud?'; 'Would you rather be a train or a boat?' This activity is often used as a skill-building game when developing Philosophy for Children (P4C) in schools.

Odd one in

"This game really tests you by getting you to look at things in lots of different ways."

This activity encourages children to be more flexible and experimental in their thinking and to realise that often there is not always one clear-cut answer to every problem.

'Odd one *out*' is a common classroom exercise for testing children's knowledge; 'odd one *in*' raises the creative challenge by encouraging children to think more for themselves rather than being passive recipients of facts. To play odd one in:

- Show the class a list of objects, animals, plants and ask the children that standard question: 'Which is the odd one out and why?' For example, rose, tulip, daffodil, aconite, ragwort, cornflower. The 'right' answer is ragwort because it is a weed (as cornflowers are now endangered they are grown as an ornamental plant in gardens).

- Now split the class into small groups and ask the children to try and find a reason why each of the other flowers could equally be the odd one out. Personal and subjective reasons count, so it's acceptable for a child to say, 'Aconite, because it's the only one I've never heard of.'

- Use the flower names as headings and list all the reasons the children offer. Ask them to think about which reasons are the strongest/ most convincing/most valid and so on.

Hypothesising

"Through this activity the children come to understand that the more information you have, the more solid is your foundation for thinking."

Asking children to practise hypothesising dampens the tendency for them to make snap judgements and jump to possibly unwarranted conclusions.

Play the 'clues' game with the children to introduce them to the concept of hypothesis.

1 Choose a 'phenomenon to be observed'. For example, Darren usually sneezes whenever he visits his friend Tony's house.
2 Now create pieces of information around that idea. Some of these will point towards possible explanations for Darren's sneezes while others will be red herrings or otherwise irrelevant. Create as many clues as you like, depending on the time available for the children to sift through the information:
   • Tony's Mum, Anita, wears a strong perfume.
   • Tony rarely tidies or cleans his room.
   • Tony's Dad grows camellias.
   • Anita's friend Sue has a dog called Fetch.
   • In Tony's lounge there is a 37" flat-screen TV.
3 Ask the children to glance through the information scraps to spot any possible clues to Darren's problem.
4 Now ask the children how they can test these possibilities. What other observations could they make/what further questions can they ask/what further experiments could they try to narrow down the reason for Darren's sneezing?

What happens next?

"Our teacher Mr Darrow says that predicting is where guessing, knowing and working-out meet."

Predicting is a versatile thinking skill that can incorporate recall, pattern recognition, prioritising, inference and reasoning. Prediction activities can also be varied endlessly in terms of the complexity of the task, and be applied to many subject areas.

Teaching tip

Once children become familiar with exercises like these they can create their own to challenge each other.

The simplest kinds of prediction simply require children to carry on a sequence that they have previously learned by rote. For example, 'a-b-c-d-?-?' or '3-6-9-12-?-?'. A degree of reasoning can be built into the task: 'a-b-d-g-k-p' or '3-6-10-15-21', and so on.

- Make the activity more complex by showing children part of a sequence then ask them to work out not just what comes next but what came before: '- ?-?-?-D-E-F-?-?'
- Build in the concept of 'analogy'-a correspondence between two ideas, where the structure or pattern of one mirrors that of another. For example, 'If Z=26, then A=?' You can take analogies further: 'Spider is to fly as cat is to ?'/'June is to July as ? is to May.'/'Whisper is to shout as walk is to ?'
- Use reasoning to find the solution. Set up simple situations where children have to predict which items match which people. For example, if the items are diary, razor, knitting-bag, chocolates, saw, grapes, fishing rod. Which person do they belong to?
  - Mr Brown, who has a beard and enjoys woodwork.
  - Mrs Brown, who is ill in bed but she can sit up and use her hands.
  - Jim Brown, who is clean-shaven and does not enjoy outdoor activities.
  - Mary Brown, who is 12 years old, loves English and has a sweet tooth.

Taking it further

Read part of a story and ask the class to decide what might happen next. Predict what computers might be like in 50 years, and so on.

The before game

"This game is fun. It's like stepping into a time machine and zooming back into the past!"

This basic technique takes just a few minutes to teach and then children can use it for themselves as a planning tool for their creative writing and as a way of reflecting on causes, effects and consequences. It also gives them a mental 'mechanism' for thinking before they act.

In the same way as the words 'fortunately' and 'unfortunately,' 'because' and 'if' and 'then' (see Ideas 72, 73 and 74 respectively), 'before' can be used as a *connective prompt*, a way of helping children to link ideas. The main purpose of the before game is to encourage children to create chronological links going backwards in time.

Begin with a vague sentence. For example, 'Jones lay slumped on the sofa,' as used elsewhere in this book. Tell the children you want them to have ideas about Jones and maybe people he knows that go back in time. Begin by saying:

> You: Before Jones lay slumped on the sofa...
> Child: He came home from work.
> You: Before he came home from work...
> Child: He went to the supermarket.

Usually children give you ideas for things that happened shortly before your previous statement. You can 'time hop' further back:

> You: A week before Jones was talking with his friend...
> Child: Jones started his new job.
> You: Two months before Jones started his new job...
> Child: He lost his old job.

As with the other connective prompt games, you are looking for spontaneous ideas from the children. This keeps the game interesting, since no one can anticipate where the 'story' will go.

The fortunately-unfortunately game

"This game is one of the quickest ways I know for developing positive thinking."

This activity takes just a few minutes. It can be used to plot stories, to explore issues for further discussion and debate and, in the longer term, to develop the life skill of controlling negative thinking.

Teaching tip

One aspect of how the mind works is that we consciously think about certain things and we subconsciously react to others. For example, if I decide to take a sip of coffee, my hand automatically (as a subconscious response) reaches for the cup. So this means that constantly thinking negative thoughts eventually sets up an unhelpful 'perceptual filter', whereby we see the world in a negative light by default, our automatic response, subconsciously, is negative. However, learning to balance negative and positive viewpoints creates a more neutral perspective and ultimately gives us the capability to have a 'fortunately-fortunately' view of life. In this regard, the fortunately-unfortunately game offers a strategy that allows children (and us!) to see the silver lining in every cloud.

Begin with an artfully vague sentence, i.e. one that offers some precise information but which also begs many questions. Let's use the old favourite: 'Jones lay slumped on the sofa.' The immediate purpose and benefit of the game is that it helps children to 'toggle' in their minds between possible positive and negative consequences, developing the habit of being able to look at something from two different points of view.

Explain to the class that at the end of the sentence you'll add the word 'fortunately' and that they have to come up with some positive consequence of Jones lying slumped on the sofa. Pick the first appropriate/reasonable idea suggested to you:

> You: Jones lay slumped on the sofa, *fortunately*...
> Child: He was catching up on his sleep.

Now ask for an unfortunate consequence, by adding 'unfortunately' to the end of the same sentence:

> You: Jones was catching up on his sleep, but *unfortunately*...
> Child: His lit cigarette caused the sofa to catch fire!

Continue adding fortunately/unfortunately to the end of each new suggestion until you feel the game has run its course:

> You: Jones's sofa caught fire [caused by the lit cigarette], but fortunately...
> Child: Jones smelt the smoke and woke up.
> You: He woke up, but unfortunately...
> Child: The smoke was so thick he couldn't find the door.
> You: He couldn't find the door, but fortunately...
> Child: A neighbour smelt the smoke and opened the door to Jones's flat.

And so the game can proceed. Either set a time limit of a few minutes for the activity, or conclude the game when the children seem to be struggling for further ideas.

Playing the fortunately-unfortunately game on a regular basis gives children more control over their thinking and proves to be especially useful for those children who habitually look on the negative side.

Taking it further

Use the maybe hand (see Idea 60) afterwards to think of other fortunately-unfortunately options at each point.

Analyse the information by using the three-step technique (see Idea 46) – What do we know? What do we think we know (assumptions and inferences)? What do we need to ask to find out?

Use the game to 'unpack' arguments for and against in a topical issue such as 'The Government has said yes to building three new nuclear power stations'.

The because game

"Mr Hemphill says that 'because' is a sticky word. Whenever you use it you have a stick a reason on the end."

This activity can be used as a plotting tool for story writing and can also help children to develop the ability to structure reasoned arguments.

Notice how the game can quickly move into topical and maybe controversial issues. You can exploit this tendency if you want the class to explore different topics for later discussion. Note too that you will need to be creative yourself in running this activity: you might need to 'tweak' a child's response to keep the game going. Also be aware that sometimes a child's response won't logically follow what has just been said, in which case you can say, 'What can you add to that to make your reason a bit stickier?'

Because this activity emphasises reasoning you can follow on with 'Be reasonable' (Idea 52). It also helps children to understand character motivation in their own and others' stories, and gives them a mental tool for thinking about consequences of their own actions – either before or after they have carried them out!

Begin with a vague sentence (see Idea 72 'The fortuntately-unfortunately game'). This time let's use: 'They shook hands but only Baxter was smiling'.

- Say the sentence to the class and tell the children that the next time you say the sentence you'll add the word 'because' at the end and that their job is to come up with a reason as to *why* only Baxter was smiling.
- Pick the first reasonable and appropriate idea suggested by the children to continue the example:

You: They shook hands but only Baxter was smiling because...
Child: He has just made a massive profit on the deal.
You: Baxter's profit was so big because...
Child: He'd bought the goods very cheaply.
You: He was able to buy the goods so cheaply because...
Child: The workers who made them were paid very little.
You: The workers were paid very little because...
Child: Paying them more would make the goods too expensive.

The if-then game

"This activity quickly helps children to think about cause, effect and consequence. It also gives them a greater grasp of how themes can be interlinked within the chosen topic."

This game develops children's powers of reasoning, links this with anticipating/predicting and offers an approach towards identifying and exploring problems as a precursor to searching for solutions.

Set up this activity in the same way as the games in Ideas 71–73. The main difference here is that rather than seeking to spark spontaneous ideas you're looking for the children's responses to be more considered.

- Base the game around a topic you want the children to think about carefully, perhaps relating it to a subject you're currently studying with them.
- To play the game, present the class with a sentence that starts with the word 'If' and ends in the word 'then' and ask the children to provide the conclusion. For example:

You: If people's thoughts actually appeared in thought bubbles over their heads, then...
Child: You'd have to be really careful what you thought about!
You: And if you needed to be so careful, then...
Child: Some people would hide themselves away so not to be seen by others.
You: And if that happened, then...
Child: There might not be enough people around to do the jobs available.

Teaching tip

Feel free to 'steer' the dialogue in what you think is the most useful direction. To the final response above you could say, 'And if there were not enough people to do the jobs in society then...' This takes the dialogue towards themes to do with the labour market and the economy. But you could take it in a different direction, for example, 'And if some people didn't mind showing off their thoughts, then...' or 'Some people might become really good at controlling their thoughts. If that happened, then...'. Notice that even when the initial scenario is impossible and fantastical, it can quickly lead into exploring 'real life' themes; the economy as we've seen, but also issues of privacy, deception, control of thoughts, etc.

Cut-ups

"I enjoy doing cut-ups, it's like doing a puzzle and doesn't feel like work at all!"

'Cut-ups' are a way to record pieces of information using small scraps of paper that groups of children arrange according to a set task. Use this activity as a precursor to the mysteries technique (Idea 89).

Cut-ups are any selection of small scraps of paper that contain various bite-sized pieces of information. The exercise can be adapted to meet the needs of a wide age and ability range by varying the number of paper scraps, the complexity of the information on each, the relationship between them and the sophistication of the task itself. An obvious benefit of the activity is that the scraps can be rearranged any number of times when the children change their minds as they work towards a solution. Some ideas to get you started include:

- Cut up a recipe and ask the children to place the steps in a logical order.
- Cut up a comic book story for groups to reconstruct.

Try leaving out some scraps with information and substitute with blank pieces of paper. Ask the children, based on what comes before and after, what they think the missing panels would look like; this works particularly well with comic strips. You can also substitute bank panels with the paragraphs of a short story. Vary the activity by leaving out the start or end. What are the children's ideas about how the story should begin and conclude?

Flip it

"You can never get a wrong answer with the coin flips game, but it does mean you have to think of good questions."

Creativity guru Edward de Bono states that creative thinking is enhanced by introducing randomness and chance into the mix. The coin flip technique is the simplest way of doing this.

'Flip it' is a simple heads-and-tails game that can be used in many ways, for example, with a picture, such as the walking man mentioned in Idea 13 (available to download from the online resources).

- Explain to the class that in order to learn more about the picture and to be able to build a story around it they can ask 'yes/no questions' (any question as long as the answer is 'yes' or 'no'). Discuss the notion of relevance and 'quality questions' beforehand. Every piece of information gathered must contribute positively to the story. If a question does not seem to satisfy the criterion, ask the child to explain their reasoning, then accept or disallow the question as appropriate.
- A child asks a question, flips the coin to get the answer, then passes the coin on to the next child. A 'yes' (heads) answer means that the children have gained a piece of information that can form the basis of further questions. A 'no' (tails) answer means that the children have to think of another idea. So, 'Is the man being chased?' – no – means that another possibility must be thought of. Several no answers to the question really begin to challenge children's creativity.
- Coin flips can be done as a whole-class activity, or children can work individually or in groups. Children should just make brief notes of yes answers.

All in order

"Prioritising is an important thinking skill for developing children's ability to analyse, organise, reason and decide."

Prioritising is the creation of an ordered sequence based on one or more criteria. The word 'criterion' derives from the Greek meaning to judge or decide.

As with many thinking skills, activities for prioritising can be widely differentiated to suit the needs of your group.

- Run simple gradation activities as a precursor to more challenging prioritisation tasks. Use one or two criteria initially. For example, based on volume: kettle, cup, tub, pail, barrel; based on size: elephant, whale, lion, ant, mouse. Extend the skill into other subject areas, for example, take elements from the Periodic Table and have the children grade them in terms of their complexity.
- Explain that some prioritised lists have one right answer given certain criteria; an ant will always come before an elephant if the criterion is 'size', smallest first. But if the criterion was 'rarity' the elephant would come first. Items can also be sorted subjectively. Ask the children each to make a list of their top five favourite foods. Look at bestseller lists in bookstores. Read some short stories or poems with the class and discuss which is the best, and by what criteria the decision is made (if it can be).
- Move on to more complex tasks. Ask them draw up a to-do list to prepare for a camping trip with friends. First, they must decide what items they want to take, but as space is limited in their rucksacks the criteria of necessity, size and weight become important.

Taking it further

Introduce or revisit the idea of diamond ranking. This is where items are not placed in a strictly linear sequence: items that are equivalent are placed side by side, so you might have one item at the top, below that two side by side, below that another three side by side, forming a rough diamond shape. Go back to the favourite foods list and find out if applying diamond ranking is a more accurate/useful way to prioritize the list.

How much do I agree?

"Doing these games made me realise that it's important to have reasons behind your decisions."

Younger children tend to see the world in terms of binary opposites: a person is tall or short, fat or thin, good or bad. However, as they grow older children come to realise that things are usually more complicated, with people, ideas, beliefs and so on, positioning themselves between those two extremes.

Draw a line on the board. At one end write 'I completely agree' and at the other 'I completely disagree'. Ask the children to write down personal statements at each end of the line. It doesn't matter how few or how many statements each child writes. Afterwards, discuss with them how difficult it was to think of ideas. Ask them now to give a reason to support each statement, for example, 'I completely agree that eating fruit is good for you because...'

Now fill in the line between the extremes: 'I strongly agree'/'I mildly agree'/'I mildly disagree'/'I strongly disagree'. Ask the children to write more statements that they could put at the end of each line, with associated reasons and qualifiers ('I strongly disagree, but with these exceptions...')

Draw a line on the board with a small triangle beneath and in the middle so it looks like a seesaw/simple balance. Put two potentially conflicting ideas at the ends, making sure it is appropriate to the age of the children, for example, for Year 5/6 group you could put 'freedom' and 'control' at either end. Where along the line would children stand? What would their version of society look like?

Teaching tip

You might find that some statements are controversial and that airing them in the class is inappropriate. To keep control, suggest the children follow neutral ideas, for example, food, for general discussion.

Thinking grids for stories

"Using the grid means I can make up stories easily whenever I like."

A thinking grid introduces the element of randomness and chance. Taking the mind 'by surprise' in this way aids creative thinking by dampening the tendency to think in a linear-sequential way.

Make a grid of 36 boxes. Choose the fiction genre you want the children to write about. Now fill the grid with pictures and words. Some of the pictures should be of things you usually find in stories of that genre, while others can be more general. The words should have a variety of meanings depending on their context. (An example 'Thriller grid' can be downloaded from the online resources.)

Here are some activities to use with the grid:

- Play the 'zig-zag story' game. Tell the children that you are going to roll a die and count that number of boxes along the top row, starting from the left-hand corner. Whichever picture/word you land on will tell you about how the story starts. Roll the die again. If it takes you to the second row, count from right-to-left. Tell the children that whichever picture you land on will tell you something about what happens next. Continue in this way, zigzagging down the board until the story is complete. You can also suggest beforehand that the last picture landed on in the bottom row will tell you something about how the story ends. This way of using the grid is more suitable for younger children. You can also cut down the size of the grid if necessary.
- The 'co-ordinates' game. This time start in the *bottom* left-hand corner. Roll the die twice to find the co-ordinates of a picture or word. Tell the class that you are going to

choose a second box and as soon as you do, the children will be able to put them together to have an idea for a story. Roll the die and pick a second box. Pick one child's contribution for demonstration purposes.

Once you have an initial idea, explain to the class that they must now come up with an open question about the story and that the next box chosen will answer that question or at least give the children a clue. For example, if a diamond and a pile of rocks were the boxes chosen, and that the story-starter idea was, 'A diamond was buried under a pile of rocks' then a suitable open question would be 'Why was the diamond buried?'

Roll the die again to select the next box and pick one child's response. Now the children have to come up with another question, which will be answered by a further dice roll. And so the game proceeds. Some children will want to keep rolling the die until it has revealed the whole plot, while others will want to stop as soon as they have worked out their story.

Bonus idea

Create a story grid based on a book you're reading with the class. Making up further adventures for the characters will help children to remember scenes from the original novel and also creates the opportunity to discuss character motivation. Children can also make their own grids based on a favourite book or film.

Thinking grids for inventing

"I asked the children to look around the classroom and told them that everything they could see had to be thought of before it could be built."

Thinking grids are not limited to story making (see Idea 79); they can be really useful when tackling big subjects, such as inventing.

Create a grid containing pictures of ordinary household items and gadgets. Explain to the class that you will be rolling the dice to choose the co-ordinates of a pair of objects. The children must find out what the two objects are and then put them together to create a new invention! (An example of a Thinking grid for inventing is available to download from the online resources.)

Emphasise to the children that it's better to keep ideas spontaneous rather than trying hard to work out a solution. In the first instance, this is a brainstorming game and the aim is to have lots of ideas in order ultimately to have the best ideas. Also, point out that at this stage the children do not have to be concerned with how their inventions would actually work!

For example, a group might come up with the following new inventions:

- Flashlight/clothes peg – luminous pegs so that you can hang out or take in your washing in the dark.
- Brush/chair – a self-cleaning chair that repels dust and animal hairs.
- Soap/key – soap that incorporates a chemical 'key' so that it will wash off dirt but not make-up.
- Teapot/cigarette lighter – a teapot with a built-in heater to keep tea warm.

Thinking grids for topics

"I remembered so much more about the Romans when we used the topic grid to make stories about them."

Topic grids can be used to help children assimilate and remember factual material from various subject areas.

Using the example of the Roman invasion of Britain, create a grid featuring pictures of Roman artefacts and relevant prompt words such as 'gods', 'border', 'invade', 'empire', 'legion', 'slave' and so on. Other relevant vocabulary including dates, names of prominent figures from that time and place names can be arranged around the grid. Encourage the children to incorporate these words into their stories as far as possible. (An example of a Roman grid is available to download from the online resources.)

In conjunction with the basic narrative elements (Idea 54 'Pyramid Planning'), children can form their plots around a number of key points that traditionally appear in stories:

- Call to action: The hero/heroine doesn't want to get involved but feels morally compelled to do so.
- First brush with danger: As the hero sets off on the journey, there is an early crisis.
- Crossing the threshold: Entering unfamiliar territory, the hero's courage is tested.
- Point of lowest ebb: After a number of crises/encounters the hero is ready to give up, but battles on!
- Point of greatest danger: Far from home, even though things seem to be going well, the hero is very vulnerable.
- Point of complacency: The hero thinks all is well until...
- Twist in the tale: A final clash with danger before the villain is defeated.

Teaching tip

Even though the children will use the grids to create 'made up' stories set at the time of the Roman invasion of Britain, the narrative gives them a context that will help them to remember actual people, places and events.

Taking it further

Topic grids can be used with younger children by playing the simpler 'zig-zag story' game, or the more sophisticated co-ordinates version with older children. One benefit of the grid technique is that all of the material is visible the whole time – children will be subconsciously assimilating images and words as they consciously work on their stories.

Thinking grids for problem solving

"If you only have a hammer you see every problem as a nail."

Sometimes problems can be solved logically and methodically, while at other times creativity and 'out of the box' thinking are required. Try using different grids as a way of prompting new and possibly useful connections.

Before running the activity, explain that objects can represent other things, for example, ideas and feelings. If we look at the Animals grid idea from Idea 44 'Twenty questions', for instance, a bull could represent rage or a bat could stand for blindness. (This is a useful opportunity to revisit similes.) Or if we look at the Thriller story grid idea from Idea 79 'Thinking grids for stories', a book could represent knowledge, a jewel could stand for wealth.

First of all clearly identify the problem to be solved. This could be a minor issue, such as how to create more storage space in your classroom or it could be a more general issue, like attracting more shoppers to the high street.

- For this activity you can use more than one grid simultaneously. Give each grid a number and roll the die once to choose which grid to consult each time.
- Tell the class that they will roll the die to obtain the co-ordinates of a box from one of the grids. This box will give them a clue to solving the problem. (Some children might actually come up with a solution after a single dice roll – in which case move on to another problem!)
- Once the box is chosen invite the children to tell you their ideas for how to solve the problem, based on the image in the box.

Emphasise that 'we need to have lots of ideas to have our best ideas': analysing and assessing the ideas comes later.

- If no ideas are offered, roll the die again to choose a second box. Tell the class that that second object will give us a clue about *how to use the first object to solve the problem*. It's important that the children don't force ideas; they'll come or they won't.
- Let's suppose the problem is how to attract more shoppers and tourists to the town. We have numbered the grids: Animal grid 1, Thriller story grid 2, Inventing grid 3, Roman grid 4.
- First dice roll, Inventing grid 3. Next dice rolls 2/6 which brings us to a box with a picture of a teapot.
  - Open more coffee shops in town.
  - Put a free hot drinks voucher in the local paper or on the town website.
  - Have an idea-sharing tea party for local people.
  - Thought association: teapot, teatime, friends round for tea, families together, family values...Think of ways to make the town friendlier and more welcoming to visitors (another dice roll called for). Promote the town as a family day out with something for everyone.
- A further dice roll to choose another grid – Animal grid 1. Next dice rolls 5/3, bring us to a dinosaur.
  - Open a dinosaur attraction in an empty shop.
  - (Dinosaur represents out-of-date thinking) What is the modern shopper looking for? How can we tempt new visitors? (Another dice roll needed).
- Choose another grid – Thriller story grid 2. Next dice rolls 4/6, bring us to a road.
  - Set up a park and ride scheme to improve access to the town.
  - Have clearer signs around the town to advertise shops people might otherwise miss.

Structure and function

"Doing this activity made me realise that things are the way they are for a reason."

'Structure and function' develops attention and observation skills, reasoning skills and generating creative insight.

Teaching tip

An implicit benefit of the activity is that it develops the habit of children actively questioning what they see around them, rather than simply not noticing things and/or just taking them for granted.

Begin by showing the class some simple objects that demonstrate the link between structure and function:

- Why are house keys different shapes?
- Why does a fork have four prongs (rather than three or six) that curve upward?
- Why are frying pans larger and flatter than saucepans?
- Why do doors usually open into a room?
- Why is the light switch usually near the door?
- Why do the slates and tiles on roofs overlap each other?
- Why does a showerhead have lots of little holes (and not a few bigger ones)?
- Why are radiators made of metal not plastic?
- Why do cats have whiskers?
- Why do we have a pullcord in the bathroom and not an ordinary light switch?
- What is the advantage of a saucepan having a plastic handle rather than a metal one?

While some or all of the reasons might seem like common sense to adults, many children will not have considered these questions before and will need to reason their way towards an answer.

Extend the activity by encouraging the class to come up with further questions about other common, everyday objects. Emphasise that it doesn't matter if children don't know the answers to the questions they pose, finding out could make an interesting research project.

Taking it further

Split the class into groups. Give each group a complicated object to think about-for example, a telescope, car, printer, computer keyboard. Ask them to examine it in detail and come up with a list of questions relating structure to function.

Thirteen ways of looking

"I learned from this activity that everyone sees things differently and in their own way."

The inspiration for this idea came from Wallace Stevens' poem *Thirteen Ways of Looking at a Blackbird*. Adapt the activity to suit the age of the children and topic area under study: obviously you don't need to stick with just thirteen responses.

Pick an object and have each child write one statement about it. For example, a Year 4 class might come up with these ideas for 'dog': 'Big, small, laid back or excited but always your friend'; 'Only bites your hand when he's cross'; 'Howls when his owner is gone'; 'Ours snores worse than my dad!'

Make the activity more sophisticated for older children. Choose a theme, split the class into groups and ask each group to invent or research a definition. For example, a Year 6 group might come up with these for 'human being': 'Someone being human'; 'A pile of chemicals once the water's removed'; 'A universe of thoughts behind the face'; 'Image of God.'

Link the activity to other subject areas. A Year 5 class might come up with these ideas when studying the topic of water and the water cycle: 'Earth crying through loss'; 'Hydrogen and oxygen holding hands. But it still tastes sweet'; 'Some people would give everything for a drink of it'; 'The greatest ocean is made out of countless raindrops'; 'Mars is alien – not a single tumbling stream'; 'Cycles endlessly, renewed and returning. There's a lesson here.'

Teaching tip

Extend the technique by choosing the focus and asking the children, for example, 'How would a scientist look at this?'; 'How would an optimist look at this?'.

Taking it further

Study Wallace Stephens' poem with the children and notice the different ways of looking. Repeat them for a different animal.

The Merlin game

"I tell the children that 'Merlin is the wizard of your imagination. Wave the wand to make things change by mental magic.'"

This technique can be used to generate story ideas, solve problems and to practise brainstorming.

Teaching tip

For younger children you can simplify the terminology for transforming things to: 'make bigger' (enlarge); 'make smaller' (reduce); 'change the shape' (stretch); 'take something away' (eliminate); 'swap something' (substitute); 'turn something around' (reverse).

The aim of the Merlin game is to transform things in a number of ways. Traditionally, these are enlarge, reduce, stretch, eliminate, substitute, reverse. A quick way of demonstrating the technique is to take a well-known story such as 'Cinderella'. Waving Merlin's wand in these ways produces:

- Enlarge: The horses and carriage don't change back/Cinderella's feet swell once she's lost the glass slipper/we could write more stories about Cinderella after the Prince finds her.
- Reduce: The Fairy Godmother only has a little bit of magic and can't help Cinderella much/the Prince has a tiny fortune, he's doing the ball on credit/write Cinderella as a mini-saga (50-word story).
- Stretch: An evil Fairy Godmother turns the glass slippers into workmen's boots/the magic goes wrong and the mice keep morphing into different animals.
- Eliminate: The Fairy Godmother makes the ugly sisters vanish/the Prince loses the slipper/Cinderella doesn't fancy the Prince and goes into hiding.
- Substitute: The ugly sisters swap the glass slipper for ones their size/the horses and carriage become a stretch limo.
- Reverse: Tell the story in flashback after Cinders and the Prince are happily married/make the sisters pretty and Cinderella ugly.

Taking it further

If you use the Merlin game as a problem-solver, select the problem, state your fixed goal or desired outcome and identify the components you want to work with. For example: Problem: 'I'm a chocolate-maker but I'm not selling much.' Fixed goal: 'I want to increase sales.' Components: The chocolate itself, packaging, advertising campaign and budget.

Story circles

"This idea has helped me to think about people, places and stories I'd like to write".

A circle template can help children to assimilate information into different areas of their learning.

We've seen how a circle template can be used to help children think about themselves, other people and characters in a story (Idea 30 'The world inside'). This allows information to be gathered and associated since the words and images are within the circle.

- The circle idea can also be used to learn about genre fiction. Children come to understand genre through its motifs and conventions. 'Motifs' are characters, objects, places, scenes and dialogue that help to describe and define the genre in question. 'Conventions' refer to those things that we would conventionally recognise as belonging to that genre. For example, a dragon is a motif found in Fantasy fiction and, conventionally, we would expect it to breathe fire or guard a treasure hoard.
- Referring to your class reader, books the children have read and films they've watched, collect motifs/conventions from one or more genres. Draw a circle on the board and label it 'Fantasy'. All the things that the children have collected could be put in that circle.
- Do the same for two or three other genres. Draw the circles on the board and allow them to overlap, like the Olympic rings. The overlapping areas are where aspects of one genre meet and mingle with those of another. If the children were to choose some motifs from these genres and put them in the overlap space, what would they pick.

What do you get if you cross...?

"Our teacher made us feel proud when she said we were the inventors of the future."

Making links between previously separate ideas is one of the cornerstones of creative thinking. Exploit this by playing 'What do you get if you cross...?', which also helps the children to develop their inventiveness and boosts their vocabulary.

Taking it further

The sheep-kangaroo cross is one example of the more general theme of cross-matching species. What other combinations can the children invent?

If you use the inventions grid, once the children have come up with two objects ask them to push the ideas further.

Encourage the children to come up with suitable names for their inventions. You can also work it the other way round by giving them made-up terms: what would these inventions look like – aquarette/ interport/cyberscribe/(to) octofy?

The inventing grid from Idea 80 encourages children to brainstorm ideas for new gadgets and devices. In that activity the brainstorming itself was an important aspect of the technique. The zig-zag game can be a follow-on from that or can form an activity in its own right, where more systematic inventiveness is called for.

- The basic 'formula' for running the activity is – 'If we cross A with B we get C – but what is C?' I often introduce the game by giving a few examples. 'What do you get if you cross a sheep with a kangaroo? A woolly jumper. I bet you've never heard that one before!'
- But then take it further. 'What *else* would we get? Sheep that could jump higher. Sheep with more powerful tails to help ward off predators. Kangaroos with wool. Perhaps hybrid animals able to live in a more diverse range of environments.'

Board games

"Board games are great for helping children to consolidate knowledge and develop their instructional writing."

Using a few simple templates children can create a wide variety of board games centred around stories they've read and factual topics they have studied.

The race game template could be a basic circuit that runs around a page, composed of straight lines punctuated with dots or spaces – it looks almost like a constellation – the idea is that you roll the dice to move along the lines to reach the dots. (A blank race game template and an example of a race game with Science Fiction motifs are available to download from the online resources.)

- Split the class into groups and ask each group to choose a genre. Give each group a blank race game template and access to simple pictures that they can cut out and paste on to the board – images from the story grid mentioned in Idea 79 work well, but children might like to cut up comics or use clip art.
- Next ask the groups to work out the penalties and rewards that will form an important part of the game. If the game is for two players, *they must be treated equally* as they make their way towards the finish point. When the penalties and rewards are complete players flip a coin to decide who goes first: dice rolls determine progress across the board.
- More complex boards can be created for more players on larger sheets of paper. Another way of increasing the sophistication of a game is to build in 'chance' cards that players pick up when they land on particular circles.

Teaching tip

Consider the board game idea for revising topics. Refer to the animals grid associated with Idea 44 'Twenty questions'. This game could be about a race through different environments where a variety of creatures are encountered. Encourage children to use the vocabulary of the topic in their instructions and chance cards.

The mysteries technique

"Trying to solve a mystery helps me to practise the different kinds of thinking I have learned about."

This technique helps to develop reasoning, discussion/listening skills and aids collaborative learning.

Taking it further

Invite groups to add extra infoscraps to the ones you've given them. Each group would need to make several copies of each infoscrap to hand out to other groups. Eventually groups can create their own mysteries from scratch.

The mysteries technique presents children with pieces of information written on scraps of paper ('infoscraps') together with a task to complete, such as a question to answer, a puzzle to solve, a conclusion to reach or an issue to explore. Groups must arrange and organise the infoscraps to complete the task: the discussion about this as well as the information itself forms an essential part of the learning.

Begin with a simple mystery using a relatively small number of infoscraps and a straightforward task. For instance, ask groups to discuss the pros and cons of introducing car-parking charges in town. The task would be for children to sift facts from opinions; to find any supporting evidence to justify opinions; to prioritise reasons according to their robustness before coming to a conclusion. The infoscraps would contain information such as:

Bonus idea ★

Extend the technique into other areas. Write infoscraps based on a story you've read: use bits of dialogue and description, summaries of key scenes. Ask groups to arrange these in narrative order and flesh out the story.

- Car-parking charges encourage people to use public transport.
- Philippa Stephens prefers using her car for reasons of personal safety.
- Traffic flow through the town has increased by 50% over the past six years.

Abandon Earth!

"This was a really exciting activity, very dramatic, and we all got involved."

This is a simulation game that draws together many of the ideas and skills in this book. It can be a simple one-session activity or a sequence of modules run over the course of several weeks.

Ask the children to imagine that (for whatever reason) the Earth will soon be uninhabitable and a number of evacuation programmes are will have to get underway soon to save everyone.

- Split the class into groups and put each in charge of planning the evacuation programmes – most importantly deciding what and who should be given priority aboard the evacuation ships. The different programmes can be themed: for example, animals, foodstuffs, culture, gadgets, machines.
- If you want a less elaborate version of the game offer the same scenario but tell each child that he/she can only bring ten things with them. What would they choose and why? Again discussion can follow around values, mutual support for fellow evacuees and so on.

Teaching tip

Children often want to go deeply into these issues, beyond the pragmatic matters for example, whether a seed bank is more valuable than a collection of art treasures. Sometimes discussion gets heated and values can clash. It's important that children justify their opinions, give reasons for their choices. If you are a P4C (Philosophy for Children) school this will already be familiar territory.

Taking it further

A variation of this activity is Noah's Ark: The ice caps are melting, sea levels are rising and humanity will need to survive for many years aboard huge ark-cities. Some land will still be above water so crops can be grown and some animals can be farmed, though there is limited space. What/who travels aboard the arks? How do you manage the scarce land resources?

Annotated notebooks

"Asking children to comment on their own work gives them a sense of value and control over their learning."

The annotated notebook idea is the written analogue of a director's commentary on a movie DVD or sports commentary on a football or tennis match, for example.

Invite the children to look back and write about work they have previously done: the work itself could be on the left hand page of an exercise book, commentary on the right.

- If children are commenting on their own stories they should bear in mind these two key questions:
  - What changes would I make now to improve this story?
  - What did I learn by writing the story that will make my next one better?
- Their responses may overlap to some extent but the emphasis of the questions is different. Bringing them to the children's attention also allows you to point out that they're not expected to get it absolutely right – even professional, bestselling authors are still learning the craft. You can also point out that elements that they feel are 'errors' actually *have the same learning value* as things they feel they've done well.
- Children may annotate their work before or after you've marked it. If afterwards, consider giving them the opportunity to ask questions and comment on *your* comments. Don't feel threatened by this: it is creative dialogue.
- When children are asked to comment on factual material, encourage them to write about what they didn't understand as well as what has now become clear.

The 1-6 scale for understanding

"This is good because you don't feel stupid if you don't really understand something."

This scale acts not only as a platform for children to ask more questions but it also serves as a useful feedback tool, allowing you to fine-tune your presentation of material to the class.

The 1-6 scale is perfect for checking the children's understanding. It can be used to check the whole the comprehension of a group or even used at an individual level. Children can indicate their degree of understanding privately in their own notebooks – they are more inclined to do this if you use the annotated notebook technique (Idea 91).

> **Teaching tip**
>
> I try never to forget that children are learners, so when a child says they don't understand I take it as an opportunity to reflect on my teaching.

- Make a poster that illustrates the six levels so that children can refer to it when they need to:

  1 I don't understand this idea/technique: I haven't tried to use it.
  2 I think I understand this idea/technique and will try to use it.
  3 I do understand this idea/technique and tried to use it.
  4 I know how to use/do this in other areas of the subject.
  5 I know how to use/do this and have tried to use it in other subjects.
  6 I know how to use/do this outside school.

- Periodically checking children's 1-6 assessments can guide you in lesson planning: a preponderance of low numbers might indicate that a topic needs to be revisited and further explanation is necessary.

New marking symbols for thinking

"I really feel good when my teacher tells me I've done some great thinking!"

Using 'thinking symbols' as part of your marking strategy adds a further dimension to the feedback you give to children's work and demonstrates to them that you value their thinking.

Consider using symbols both to emphasise the thinking the children have done in producing their work, and to encourage them to reflect further on their ideas. For example:

- A looped arrow – 'Look again. What else can you find out?'
- A thought bubble – 'I like the way you've thought this through.'
- Light bulb – 'Good idea!'
- Speech marks – 'Clear use of language.'
- OP tick – 'Well done, you've given reasons to back up your opinions.'

You can create a sheet of symbols with their corresponding meanings (an example sheet is available to download from the online resources for this book). Make copies for the children to keep in their books, use as a wall display or print copies on to sheets of stickers. This makes the use of the symbols quick and easy.

Thought for the day

"I like 'thought for the day'. Our teacher always makes some time for us to think and talk about it."

This simple strategy takes very little time to establish yet has great educational value not only by drawing together many of the thinking skills mentioned in this book but also making clear the essential point that the children's thinking is valued.

A thought for the day is a simple but inspirational quote. Select one quote at a time, display it prominently and give children the chance to talk about it. Change it regularly. Invite the children to suggest quotations for themselves. Quotes don't need to be 'motivational' but might be chosen to stimulate discussion or prompt further questions. Here are some that I've found work well:

- 'Technology has got us into this mess and technology will get us out of this.'
- 'When someone points at the moon, the fool looks at the finger but the wise one looks at the moon.' Traditional Chinese proverb.
- 'To remain a pupil is to serve your teachers badly.' Friedrich Nietzsche.
- 'The only high road to success is failure.' R. L. Stevenson.
- 'Don't learn it, get used to it.' Japanese proverb.
- 'As soon as you have an idea – laugh at it.' Lao Tzu.

Teaching tip

I once saw a classroom with walls decorated with lots of 'inspirational' quotes. To paraphrase one of them, 'Aim for the moon. If you miss, you'll fall among the stars.' One boy who had noticed this said, cynically, 'Or you'll fall back to Earth and burn up in the atmosphere!' Not only did the opportunity never arise to talk about this and the other quotes, but also they were simply dull photocopied sheets with curling corners, fixed high up on the walls and rarely replaced. For the thought of the day to be of value it must be discussed, explained, used and changed regularly.

A treasure box of ideas

"I'm always pleased when my idea is picked out of the box, but the other children's ideas are interesting too.'

A key element of successfully developing thinking skills is to value the children's thinking. This is easily achieved with the treasure box idea.

Several of the techniques in this book necessitate using one child's idea even though a number of children will have contributed their thoughts. In the story grid game for instance (Idea 79) in demonstrating the technique, if you try to incorporate several children's thoughts it will complicate matters. To prevent children from feeling devalued – which may dampen their willingness to take part in future – suggest that they note their thoughts down and put them in 'the treasure box of ideas'.

The treasure box might be an actual box – colourfully decorated and prominently visible in the classroom – or you might use the term metaphorically to mean that children note their idea down in their books for future use.

Another occasion where ideas are frequently 'discarded' is when you use the maybe hand technique (Idea 60) with the coin flip technique (heads or tails) or dice rolls to select one idea from those offered. Tell the children whose ideas are not picked to jot them down and put them in the treasure box of ideas.

When the children are not around, sift through the ideas so that you can mention or use some of them subsequently. You can also set up more than one treasure box. One box might be for ideas for storymaking, another ideas to do with inventing, and so on.

Skills checklist

"The checklist quickly lets me see what I can do well, and where I need to improve."

The skills checklist is a versatile tool: skills can be added as they are practised, and can be monitored by the children themselves as well as providing useful data for you on their progress.

Create a template with around a dozen boxes on an A4 sheet. In each box write the name of the skill you want the child to reflect on, with enough room for a question, a note of when/where the skill was used, an insight about that way of thinking. Some useful entries on the template are:

- I have explained an idea clearly.
- I have listened carefully to others.
- I have given a reason for my opinion.
- I have agreed/disagreed with someone and given my reason(s) why.
- I have questioned what someone else has said (using the Six Big Important Questions).
- I have kept to the main point of the discussion.
- I have built on/added to other people's opinions.
- I have given an example/counterexample.
- I have added a 'what if' to the discussion.
- I have added an 'if...then...' to the discussion.
- I have asked a question about someone else's question.

Additions to the template can also be based on specific ways of thinking: I have observed something carefully/I have checked a fact for myself/I have contributed X ideas to a maybe hand (Idea 60)/I have suggested an arrangement for some of the infoscraps in a mystery (Idea 89).

Taking it further

The skills checklist could also incorporate or be based on Bloom's Taxonomy of Thinking, which grades thinking from 'lower order thinking demonstrating little understanding' to 'higher order thinking demonstrating greater understanding' (see *Thinking for Learning*, by Mel Rockett and Simon Percival, 2002). So under the heading of 'Comprehension' – I can restate an idea/I can summarise an idea or topic/I can explain what is significant in this topic.

Knowledge to know-how

"Establishing a thinking skills classroom makes you realise how much more there is to learning than just remembering facts."

Bloom's Taxonomy for Thinking provides both teachers and children with a useful and powerful way of understanding and monitoring the development of thinking skills.

Teaching tip

Bloom's 'hierarchy' begins with relatively simple ways of thinking supported by little understanding and moves towards more sophisticated thinking supported by greater understanding. His ideas have been misinterpreted in the past to suppose that only 'brighter' children can operate at the higher levels of thinking. Practising thinking skills with your class will show you that all children can become more effective, creative and independent thinkers.

Bloom's Taxonomy for Thinking was devised by Benjamin Bloom in the 1950s. Basically, it is a system for classifying different levels of thinking. It provides both teachers and children with a useful and powerful way of understanding and monitoring the development of thinking skills. The levels of thinking included in Bloom's model are knowledge, comprehension, application, analysis, evaluation and synthesis. (For a detailed breakdown of these, see the online resources.)

To apply Bloom's model in your classroom:

- Reflect on your current classroom practice to check that 'higher order' thinking tasks are used in conjunction with your coverage of the curriculum.
- Explain Bloom's model to the children. Point out to individual children and groups the kind/level of thinking they are doing as they attempt particular tasks.
- Pin the ideas and techniques in this book to Bloom's model. Help your class to understand how creativity, speculation, inference and so on lead them towards higher order thinking.

Effective learners

"Our teacher Mrs Kirkman told us that 'effective' means 'powerful'. That made us all feel good about ourselves."

Part of the power of helping children to think for themselves is that it changes their attitude towards learning, towards themselves, others and the world around them.

As they become more creative and independent thinkers, children are no longer simply 'learners' but are increasingly able to 'learn *how to* learn' (one of the central mantras of the Accelerated Learning approach to education).

Look out for these indicators of effective learning and let the children know you have noticed them. As the wise old saying goes, 'Catch them doing something well – and tell them.'

Effective learners:

- come to see themselves and others differently
- accept themselves and their feelings fully and increasingly become more emotionally resourceful and able to use all emotions more positively
- become more independent and self-directing in many ways, including how they tackle their learning challenges
- become more flexible in their perceptions (can see things in different ways) and so become more considered in their judgements
- adopt realistic goals that are more in tune with their increasing capabilities. This is often linked with an increased willingness to try.

Teaching tip

In line with the general principle of 'making the thinking explicit', point out to children when you notice them engaged in effective learning behaviours and encourage them to notice such behaviours in themselves and their classmates. Ask them to use their observation journals (Idea 11) to write down their observations and reflections on their own thinking.

Our amazing minds

"Establishing a thinking skills classroom helps us to stop taking our amazing minds for granted."

The ideas in this book have dealt mainly with thinking skills themselves, and although links have been made with various subject areas you will find that these skills can be applied in all areas of the children's learning.

Teaching tip

Familiarise children with the 'vocabulary of thinking', explaining various terms they might not already understand – analogy, assumption, bias etc. Encourage the children to come up with their own examples. Devote a little time to 'make the thinking explicit'; to look at and talk about examples of the different kinds of thinking taken from a variety of sources.

The human mind is capable of a huge range of different ways of thinking. Create a poster to help familiarise children with these. Reflect on how they can become part of your classroom practice: consider how various thinking skills underpin the delivery of knowledge in the coverage of the curriculum.

Some thinking skills (in alphabetical order) to include in your poster are:

- Assuming: coming to a conclusion without evidence or reason, or with minimal evidence. Use the three-step technique (Idea 46) to help children notice assumptions: what do I know? What do I think I know? What can I ask to find out more?
- Associating: making links between ideas to create further information, to understand relationships and to create new thoughts. Creative linking is one of the basic skills for effective thinking.
- Attributing: linking qualities and traits to things.
- Bias: 'slanting' or weighting statements in a particular direction in order to support an opinion and to persuade others to take the same viewpoint. Analysing for bias involves looking for emotive and rhetorical language, generalisations and unsupported claims. Raise children's awareness of this by looking at newspaper articles and reader-comments on news websites, where bias is often obvious!

- Brainstorming: the act of letting ideas flow freely without judgement or analysis in response to a prompt or stimulus. Brainstorming is a classic tool for generating ideas as raw material that can be looked at, analysed and modified later. Make children familiar with the notion of 'How many ideas can we have and what use can we make of them?' The first stage uses brainstorming, the second one critically focussed thinking.
- Classifying: putting items into patterns, sequences or categories based on shared characteristics.
- Comparing and contrasting: looking for similarities and differences between things.
- Decision making: choosing a course of action based on rational thinking but also intuition and 'gut feelings'.
- Determining cause and effect: looking for relationships between events through time.
- Generalising: creating an overview or seeing the 'bigger picture' based on varying numbers of more detailed examples.
- Hypothesising: creating a possible but tentative explanation of how something might work based on some evidence.
- Inferring: coming to a conclusion based on reasonably robust evidence. Seeing patterns, sequences etc. based on a number of observed examples.
- Inventing: creating new ideas and applications, often through insight or by making fresh connections.
- Personifying: giving objects, animals plants human attributes.
- Predicting: noticing patterns and sequences to work out what follows.
- Prioritising: putting items in rank order based on chosen criteria.
- Problem solving: using a range of ways of thinking to overcome obstacles, resolve situations, make decisions etc.
- Visualising: the ability to create mental scenarios that may have nothing to do with the immediate circumstances.

Taking it further

Create a wall display featuring concise definitions of the terms plus a few examples. Leave space for children to add examples of their own.

I know I can think because...

"Thinking is what it's all about. Depending on how we do it, thinking can shut us in or open up our world."

In Idea 96 we looked at a skills checklist. Following on from this, create an 'attitude checklist' for your classroom.

In Idea 96 we looked at a skills checklist.

Taking it further

The primary aim of developing thinking skills is not just to help children achieve and attain more in school, but to fulfil their potential more generally in life. Create opportunities for children to talk about their experiences outside school and how the 'thinking toolkit' you have helped them to develop has brought further and wider benefits.

As the children in your class develop this attitude in the environment you have established they will come to relish challenge, enjoy thinking more and more, celebrate their own and others' achievements and fulfil their potential as learners.

Happy thinking!

An attitude checklist is a list that you can turn into a poster or wall display. You might also let children have copies of it so that they can monitor and appreciate their progress. On the poster write, 'I know I can think because' and include the following attitudes:

- 'I am curious, adventurous and playful.'
- 'I like to wonder about things and explore ideas.'
- 'I enjoy thinking of explanations for myself, but I also like to learn more about other people's explanations.'
- 'I like to be clear and precise. If I'm not sure I ask. But also I'm happy to work things out and don't feel I need to know "the right answer right now".'
- 'I value ideas and I appreciate the reasons behind things.'
- 'I like to take time to think and I appreciate being able to notice my own thoughts.'
- 'I feel more confident about myself and don't feel personally criticised, even if, in the end, my idea isn't used or my answer is incorrect.'
- 'I don't feel ignorant or stupid when I ask questions.'
- 'I like to look further into my own opinions and why I have them. I feel prepared to change my opinions if necessary.'
- 'I know that others can disagree with my opinion but they still respect me as a person. I can disagree with what other people say and respect them.'